# GETTING READY TO TEACH FIFTH GRADE

## Written by Susan Cloud Marino

## Photos by Bruce Hazelton

## Illustrated by Anita DuFalla

Rosalie Cochran

Michael Cairns

We warmly thank the community of the Fern Avenue School of Torrance, California, especially Mrs. Rosalie Cochran, principal; Mr. Michael Cairns, fifth-grade teacher; and students, parents, and caregivers of Mr. Cairn's fifth-grade class.

Project Manager: Barbara G. Hoffman

Editor: Kaori Crutcher

Book Design: Anthony D. Paular

Cover Design: Anthony D. Paular

Pre-Press Production: Daniel Willits

FS122007 Getting Ready to Teach Fifth Grade
All rights reserved—Printed in the U.S.A.
23740 Hawthorne Blvd.
Torrance, CA 90505

> Let us put our minds together and see what life we can make for our children.
>
> —Tatanba Iotanko (Sitting Bull) 1877

# CHAPTER ONE: INTRODUCTION

# THE FIFTH-GRADE STUDENT

Fifth grade is a memorable year for students. This book is designed to help you create an outstanding fifth grade program. It was written with love for all of my students and my two sons. It was also written out of respect for all those teachers who have shared their talents and valuable secrets with me.

One of my favorite cookbooks has this inspiring quote by John Ruskin: "When love and skill work together, expect a masterpiece." With your help and guidance, your students will be able to create many masterpieces this year. I hope this book helps to make teaching fifth grade a memorable experience for you!

Susan Marino

During fifth grade, students generally have their tenth or eleventh birthdays. Typical students in fifth grade:

- are very talkative and enjoy working in groups

- come to school to be with their friends

- prefer friends of the same sex, but may display interest in the opposite sex by teasing

- differ as to physical development—girls tend to be taller than the boys

- are competitive and enjoy games

- have a high energy level and require frequent opportunities for movement and physical activity

- often change rules to suit the present situation

- have a naive interpretation of fairness

- compare students' abilities in particular school subjects and in sports

- have a strong feeling of community and work well in cooperative groups

- often have best friends and may purposefully exclude another student from their group

- enjoy reading both for pleasure and to gain information

- are starting to develop conceptual skills and will give opinions when asked

- are able to see similarities and can be very logical in their thinking

- have a need to understand the "why" behind everything

- are very willing to research facts and ready to learn facts

- are excited about new projects

- are developing strong study skills

- are able to take on new responsibilities

- are able to understand the relationship between cause and effect

- enjoy themselves, their family, and their friends

- may use inappropriate language

- understand the reason for rules and will willingly participate in establishing behavior guidelines for their class

- like their teacher and want him or her to be fair, soft-spoken, able to laugh at their sense of humor, and to help them gather the skills that will help them survive puberty and middle school

**TIP!**

*Identify your students' strengths and build on them.*

# OVERVIEW OF THE FIFTH-GRADE CURRICULUM

This section is presented in alphabetical order by content area. The sequence is Language Arts, Mathematics, Multicultural Education, Physical Education, Science and Health, Social Studies, Technology, and Visual Arts and Music.

In this overview section, you will read about the concepts that are to be addressed in fifth grade. In Chapter Two—Bringing the Curriculum to Life—you will find a list of skills by content area generally accepted as appropriate for fifth grade. Following the lists of skills, you will find activities that you can use to teach the skills.

The content and curriculum information presented in this book is provided as a reference. It is not intended to replace your school or district's course of study or curriculum guides. As additional references, you should read the standards published by national teacher organizations such as the National Council of Teachers of Mathematics (NCTM). Your school or district resource centers will probably have copies of the National Standards documents you can use as references.

Parts of the curriculum sections of this book are based on the Standards of the National Council of the Teachers of Mathematics, the National Council of the Teachers of English, and the National Research Council of the National Academy of Sciences. Other references used are state frameworks and school district curricula from California, Illinois, Massachusetts, Nebraska, New York, and Washington.

## Language Arts

Language Arts is a broad area of the curriculum which includes listening, thinking, speaking, writing, and reading. These processes enable students to make connections between information they know and information they don't know.

The language arts are integrated process skills that help students move into higher levels of critical thinking. The ability to communicate ideas both orally and in writing is the focus of language arts in fifth grade.

Your school or district may have adopted textbooks or other language arts programs that include grammar, spelling, workbooks, or other specific guidelines you are expected to follow. Check with the curriculum coordinator or principal at your school before the school year begins.

### Concepts

• Language is used to communicate ideas.

• Language allows us to express our life experiences, to better understand and share ourselves with others, and to provide names and labels to what we know and value.

• How language is used shapes the course of events. Most new vocabulary words come into regular use through major conflicts, through changing technologies, and through the sciences.

Three components are important to developing the art of language in your classroom. The first is the role of literature, the second is the role of writing as a process, and the third is access to educational media resources.

The first component, literature, has the power to bring the world to life. Literature may be used to introduce and support thematic units, to extend new ideas and information into different contexts, and to supply important subject area information and stimulate curiosity about a new subject.

Writing as a process, the second component, is an essential part of language development. The stages of the writing process include prewriting, drafting, receiving responses, revising, editing, and in most cases, postwriting. Through the writing process students develop their writing and communication skills by concentrating on what they want to say, deciding how to say it, and choosing to make changes to form or content if needed.

The third important component to developing the art of language in your classroom is the use of library media resources. Your students should have regular access to a variety of multimedia materials from which they can select according to their own interests. You will need to develop a classroom library as well as use the resources of the school and local public libraries. These resources are necessary for fifth graders to help them develop the essential research skills they will use for a lifetime.

> **Learn as much by writing as by reading.**
> —Lord Acton

## Processes

The Language Arts are integrated process skills that help students develop communication and higher level critical thinking skills. The following are effective ways to promote concept development:

- Use cooperative groups to enable exchanging of ideas and information through summarizing, sharing, and comparing of ideas.

- Provide opportunities to generate spelling words and vocabulary lists through both extended and recreational reading assignments.

- Offer a wide selection of literature choices including folklore, poetry, realistic fiction, historical fiction, and non-fiction to satisfy a fifth grader's natural curiosity to learn.

### TIP!

*Students will be more willing to share the books they are reading if they can talk about them openly in a small, friendly group.*

Lessons which focus on the students' abilities to construct a response instead of choosing a single answer are an important aspect of math in this grade. Fifth-grade students are able to work independently as well as with others on projects that encourage both thinking and communicating. Students should be encouraged to use mathematical tools such as rulers, calculators, manipulatives, scratch paper, and arts and crafts supplies to solve problems.

## Concepts

- Numbers can be used to describe quantities and relationships between them. A number can be described in terms of how many of each group there are in a series of groups and each group in the series is a fixed multiple of the next smaller group.

- The four basic operations are used to obtain numerical information and are related to one another.

- Statements about what is known allow conjectures and conclusions to be examined in a logical fashion. Logical arguments can be used to reach a conclusion.

- Real objects and abstract shapes have features which can be compared and analyzed.

- Geometric shapes have specific attributes for which they are identified, classified, and named. Geometric shapes can be described in terms of their relationships with other shapes.

- Through measurement, one can attach a number to a quantity using a unit which is chosen according to the properties of the quantity being measured.

- The size of what is to be measured determines the appropriate measuring tool to use.

## Mathematics

In fifth grade, students explore logic, geometry, measurement, patterns and functions, statistics and probability, algebra, and number concepts. Your students will develop problem-solving strategies through lessons that give opportunities to reason, communicate, and solve problems.

- Once the rule used to generate a pattern is identified, one is able to extend the pattern indefinitely.

- Data can be organized and summarized in a variety of ways. Inference made from a set of data can be invalid due to one or more reasons. Various strategies may be used to figure out why some outcomes are more likely than others.

- Variables can be used to express a set of numerical relationships. As long as the same change is made to both quantities, an equality relationship between the two quantities remains.

## Multicultural Education

Multicultural Education is an interdisciplinary subject that should be part of the everyday curriculum. The concepts can be included in any lesson that you present. The goal of Multicultural Education is to help students develop positive attitudes about themselves and others. The fifth-grade multicultural education curriculum includes the study of self-identity, diversity, and interpersonal relations. By providing an anti-biased curriculum, your students will learn to appreciate, respect, and value differences.

### Concepts
- Each of us has a wide range of identities including gender, age, nationality, ethnicity, class, and religious affiliation.

- Americans are people who were born in, become citizens of, or live in the United States.

- Conflict may arise when there is contact between cultural groups who have different beliefs and values.

- The United States is made up of people of many different cultural groups.

- People of diverse ethnic and cultural backgrounds have greatly contributed to the development of the nation in a wide range of fields including business, education, government, sports, science, media, and the arts.

- Each person has dignity and worth. All have feelings that we can learn to recognize. Recognizing the feelings of others and reacting to them in positive ways can reduce conflict and create peace.

- Prejudice is a learned behavior. A prejudiced person does not tolerate differences. Many people in the United States have experienced prejudice and discrimination.

## Physical Education

Concepts in motor skills, physical fitness, self-image, social behavior, and recreational interest are addressed in fifth grade. Through practice, team games, relays, and dance activities, students will have an opportunity to improve self-image. In fifth grade, lessons should involve more complex manipulative and rhythmic skills. As students improve their eye-hand and eye-foot coordination, they will experience better accuracy and speed with sports equipment. Provide many opportunities for cooperative games which allow everyone to participate. There should be an emphasis placed on strategy and acceptance of the outcome of a game.

**A good teacher remembers what it's like to be a child.**

## Concepts

- Motor skills can be perfected by practicing correct techniques.

- Physical fitness levels can be increased by the use of exercise. Strength in arm and shoulder muscles can be strengthened by using circular traveling rings. By following health principles related to exercise and cleanliness, illness may be prevented.

- All people have different physical abilities. Self-knowledge can be developed by learning the importance of setting goals and working to achieve them. With focused practice, success may be attained.

- Everyone's effort is necessary to achieve group goals. Teaching a skill to a group of peers can benefit both the group and the demonstrator.

- Participating in a variety of recreational activities is a positive use of time. It's important to learn to plan appropriate leisure activities.

# Science and Health

### Science

Most state education standards and frameworks are written based on the National Science Education Standards (NSES). The NSES presents its content standards by grade ranges, K–4, 5–8, and 9–12. Consequently, specific fifth-grade science study topics vary considerably from state to state and district to district. The NSES 5–8 content standards published in 1996 follow. The science curriculum of your school or district will most likely be written to reflect these content standards.

> **TIP!**
>
> *Be sure to have plenty of workspace and equipment available so that everyone can participate.*

### *Unifying Concepts and Processes*
- Systems, order, and organization

- Evidence, models, and explanation

- Change, constancy, and measurement

- Evolution and equilibrium

- Form and function

### *Science as Inquiry*
- Abilities necessary to do scientific inquiry

- Understandings about scientific inquiry

### *Physical Science*
- Properties and changes of properties in matter

- Motions and forces

- Transfer of energy

### *Life Science*
- Structure and function in living systems

- Reproduction and heredity

- Regulation and behavior

- Populations and ecosystems

- Diversity and adaptations of organisms

### *Earth and Space Science*
- Structure of the Earth system

- Earth's history

- Earth in the solar system

### *Science and Technology*
- Abilities of technological design

- Understandings about science and technology

### *Science in Personal and Social Perspective*
- Personal health

- Populations, resources, and environments

- Natural hazards

- Risks and benefits

- Science and technology in society

### History and Nature of Science
Science as a human endeavor

- Nature of science

- History of science

### Sample Curriculum

In fifth grade, students use the scientific process to investigate, analyze, classify, and study hands-on investigations. Students investigate the relationships of organs to body systems as well as animal and plant cell structures. Students classify matter by both chemical and physical characteristics. Students investigate the conversion of energy from one form to another as well as changes in matter. Objects in space are analyzed during a study of the solar system.

Below you will find a sample curriculum frequently presented in fifth grade.

### Physical Science

- Matter can be classified by its chemical and physical properties.

- Matter consists of atoms which are the building blocks of matter.

- Matter occurs as pure substances and mixtures. Pure substances can undergo chemical and physical changes.

- A change in the atomic structure of molecules is called a chemical change.

- Energy can be used to change the state of matter.

- Energy can be converted from one form to another.

- Simple and complex machines use mechanical energy to do work.

- An electric current produces a magnetic field around a conductor as it moves through it.

> **Learning science is something that students do, not something that is done to them. "Hands-on" activities are not enough. Students must have "minds-on" experience as well.**
>
> **—National Science Education Standards**

### Life Science

- Living organisms are made up of one or more cells. Plant and animal cells have both similar and different characteristics.

- Animals can be classified by behavioral and structural characteristics.

- The organs of the human body form systems that carry on certain body functions.

- Plants and animals are adapted by behaviors, functions, and structures to survive in certain environments.

- Fossils give evidence that many species have become extinct over time and new species have come into being.

### Earth Science

- The solar system is made up of spheres of matter that revolve around the sun.

- As the Earth rotates on its axis, it also revolves around the sun, which causes specific climactic changes.

- Rocks are classified by the process in which they were formed.

- Minerals are classified according to specific properties.

- Erosion and weathering act on minerals and rocks to create soil, change landforms, and affect human activities.

- A variety of influences such as the moon, affect tides, currents, and waves.

- Earthquakes and some volcanoes occur along fault lines and release large amounts of energy and change landforms.

## Health

Health is an interdisciplinary subject that can be studied as part of your language arts, math, science, and art programs, as well as a separate unit of study. Concepts in personal health, family health, nutrition, emotional health, use and misuse of substances, diseases and disorders, environmental health, and safety are addressed in fifth grade. Students are provided with opportunities that help them understand the positive and negative consequences of risk-taking behavior and to make choices that will enhance their physical, social, and emotional well-being.

### Concepts

- Personal good health is more desirable than illness and it requires a life-long investment to achieve it. A balanced combination of physical activities, rest, recreation, and adequate diet contributes to cardiovascular health and fitness.

- Proper protection and care for eyes, ears, mouth, teeth, gums, and posture promote good general health.

- Each family member affects the health of all members of the family. Both environment and heredity interact to influence the development of living organisms. Understanding human growth and development can lead to the appreciation of oneself and others.

- The ability to adjust to, understand, and respect others will improve one's interpersonal relationships.

- Sexual behavior has significant implications for the individual and society. (This topic usually requires parental consent.)

- Daily food intake is essential to attain optimal health. Food choices are affected by life styles, peers, and individual family resources.

**TIP!**

*Are kids bringing less-than-healthy snacks to school? Try sending home a snack idea list!*

- Getting along with others, making friends, and liking oneself are essential to emotional health. Coping with and understanding emotions in an acceptable way is healthy while having unresolved conflicts causes stress and anxiety.

- Some substances are beneficial when used properly, but can seriously disrupt normal body functions when misused. Drugs are substances that change the way the body and mind work. Social and personal pressures influence one's behavior to use or not use substances. Individuals determine and choose appropriate alternatives to the use and misuse of substances.

- Many factors contribute to the causes of disorders and diseases. How much we can control and prevent disease varies.

- Individuals are responsible for their own health and for knowing when to seek help from others. The community provides health resources to protect and promote individual, family, and community health.

- There are many opportunities for careers in the health field. A relationship exists between human health and the quality of the environment. We must all work to create and maintain a safe and healthful environment.

- Many accidents can be prevented. Potential hazards need to be identified and corrected to prevent accidents. Each of us needs to be prepared to act effectively in times of emergency, including life-threatening situations. Safety can help reduce accidents and save lives.

**We're all a family under one sky.**
—Ruth Pelham

## Social Studies

The goal of a balanced elementary social studies program is to prepare students to participate in society with the knowledge, skills, and civic values to be actively and constructively involved. Fifth-grade students study United States history and geography. The focus is on the development of a new nation with immigrants from all over the world. Students will learn about the building of a new society based upon the ideal of self-government and about the experiences of different racial, religious, and ethnic groups in the United States. The study includes an appreciation for the contributions and achievements of all groups.

### Concepts

- The contributions of different groups influenced the development of our nation as we know it today. Native Americans lived throughout North America long before the explorers came. Early settlers came to this country seeking religious freedom and economic opportunity.

- The expansion of settlers westward affected the rights and lives of the Native Americans.

- Language, religion, social customs, beliefs, values, traditions, and family structure make up a group's culture. The encroachment of the European culture upon the existing Native American culture caused hardship and conflict.

- The diverse geography of the new nation offered abundant natural resources and determined where settlements developed.

- Barter as a system of trade regulated the distribution of scarce resources in the production of goods and services.

- Our democratic form of government came out of a desire for freedom of choice.

- America as a nation is made up of descendents of many cultures, races, religions, and ethnic groups.

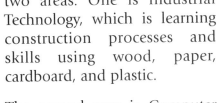

**TIP!**

*Be competent with the computer curriculum and the software selected by your district before you take students into a lab setting.*

- The principles of democracy are defined in the constitution which guarantees a separation of powers, a representative government, and a system of checks and balances.

- Citizens who took individual responsibility for ethical behavior and had a commitment to democratic values in their social behavior laid the foundation for a democratic society.

## Technology

Technology is defined as knowing how to use tools, machines, materials, techniques, and technical systems to satisfy human needs and wants. Technology can be broadly divided into two areas. One is Industrial Technology, which is learning construction processes and skills using wood, paper, cardboard, and plastic.

The second area is Computer Technology, which is learning fundamental computer tools and concepts. This arena is changing as fast as computer technology is. States and school districts are developing their academic standards in this field as this book goes to press.

## Concepts

- Technology employs both physical and mental skills.

- Interpretation of data, proper and safe use of materials, tools, and processes are necessary to successfully complete a project.

- Computer and manipulative skills improve through regular use.

- Technology consists of communication, transportation, and production.

# Visual Arts and Music

## Visual Arts

Concepts in aesthetic perception, creative expression, visual arts heritage, and aesthetic valuing are addressed in fifth grade. In order to allow opportunities for growth, students need to have activities that are planned in sequence.

### *Concepts*

- The world can be perceived and described with images and symbols having visual and tactile qualities. Visual and tactile qualities are evident in works of art, nature, events, and objects in the environment.

- Artistic knowledge and skills are necessary to express and communicate responses to experiences. Personal experiences and originality are important in expressing visual arts. Visual arts media can be used to translate ideas, feelings, and values.

- Art reflects, records, and shapes history and plays a role in every culture. Studying art leads to an appreciation of the accomplishments of others.

- Through the visual arts, people can gain an understanding of their creative abilities and artistic heritage. Understanding one's own aesthetic values can lead to an appreciation of the aesthetic values of others.

- Using objective criteria for analysis, interpretation, and judgement can lead to informed responses to art and improved art production.

## Music

Concepts in rhythm, melody, form, harmony, and expressive elements are addressed in fifth grade. Students enjoy singing and playing instruments and are exposed to a wide variety of musical styles. Many students may be involved with the school chorus or orchestra.

### *Concepts*

- The rhythm of music flows on a recurring steady beat. It consists of longer and shorter sounds and silences and is divided into sets of accented and unaccented beats or pulses. Meter is the organization of beats in groups of twos and threes. Syncopation results when accents occur on unaccented beats. Several different rhythm patterns may be performed at the same time.

- A melody is made up of tones with higher or lower pitches, that may change up or down or repeat. A feeling of repose is created when a melody ends on the home tone. Visual symbols can be used to show the relationships which can exist among tones. Tones in a melody may go up or down by step (scale) or skip (chord). A scale is a specific consecutive arrangement of tones. Melodies may be repeated beginning on different pitches. Melodies may be played or sung in a higher or lower key.

The phrase (a musical thought) is the basic unit of form in music. Identical phrases contribute to the unity of a song. A song or other composition may have an introduction, interlude, and coda. Contrasting phrases provide variety in compositions. Phrases may be partly the same and partly different. A composition with two sections is called two-part or binary form. A composition with three sections, the last a repeat of the first, is called three-part or ternary form. In rondo form, the initial section of a composition alternates with contrasting sections. Theme and variation form consists of a melody followed by several restatements with alterations or changes.

Songs can be performed with or without accompaniment. Harmony is created when two or more tones are sounded at the same time. A musical composition may be either major or minor depending upon its melody and

> **It is the supreme art of the teacher to awaken joy in creative expression and knowledge.**
>
> —**Albert Einstein**

harmony. Melodies may be combined resulting in a harmonic texture called polyphony. A chord consists of three or more tones sounded simultaneously. Harmony may apply to successions of chords. The tonic or I (one) chord creates a feeling of resolution or repose. The dominant or V (five) and the subdominant or IV (four) are active chords needing resolution when compared to the tonic chord.

- Sound is produced in diverse ways and can be modified. Tempo is relative rather than absolute. Music can move in a fast tempo and a slow tempo. Dynamics in music can be louder or softer. Changes of tempo and dynamics provide a source of variety and expressive meaning in a composition. Characteristic qualities of sounds are determined by the types of voices or instruments which produce them.

# CHAPTER TWO: BRINGING THE CURRICULUM TO LIFE

## LESSON PLANNING

Lesson planning is crucial to effectively organize your instruction. Some schools and districts require you to follow the teachers' manuals of commercial textbook series. If your district does not require this, you will be responsible for planning your instructional year. There are as many ways to plan as there are teachers—so there is no "right" way. The following is a guide.

Planning a dinner party is like planning your program of instruction. You know how many people you have invited, you know where you're going to hold the party, you have a certain time frame in mind, and you know that you are going to serve dinner. First, you must decide the presentation of your meal: Will it be formal or informal? Sit-down dinner or buffet? Based on that decision you decide what the menu of your meal will be—a meal traditional to your family and culture, or an ethnic meal? Do you want each food course to be completely different, or do you want the meal to have some unifying elements? Once you know the menu, you find the recipes to review the ingredients and preparation steps. Then you schedule your purchases and preparation time. Once the dinner is prepared, you assess your results by tasting what you prepared, watching people eat the meal, and seeing what is left over.

You can think of lesson planning in the same way as planning the dinner party. You know how many students you have, you know where you are going to teach them, and you know you are going to teach them the content and skills your school or district requires over the year. (You will find this information in your school or district's curriculum guide or course of study. Ask your principal for a copy of the curricular requirements as soon as you can.) You know that you need to organize all the information you must teach into a time frame—the school year.

Think about the concepts you want to teach over the next term. Decide what themes (the *presentation* of your school year) will provide good frameworks for these concepts. Choose themes that will interest you and your students, that are not too narrow in focus. Decide what kinds of projects (the *menu*) will give your students many opportunities to learn and practice their learning. Projects can include anything from reading 30 pages in the textbook to converting your classroom into an imaginary rain forest. Then create, select, or choose activities (*recipes*) that will support the themes and promote the learning and practice of skills (*ingredients*). Decide how many weeks (or days) you will need to accomplish your projects.

Now that you know what you want to accomplish, you need to plan how you will accomplish your long-term plans. Your weekly and daily lesson plans are the way to organize your activities into a feasible schedule. A lesson plan book will be a useful purchase if your school or district does not provide one.

Make detailed plans and schedule your instruction a week in advance. Include any regular or unusual events in the plan, such as school assemblies, class visitors, library visits, or short school days. Decide what lessons you want to include in the week and fit them into your schedule.

For your daily plans, you will want to balance activities that require sitting with activities where your students can move around more. To begin the year, you should assume that 30 minutes is long enough to require a student to stay focused on the same thing. As you get to know the students better, you will find what time frame works best for them. You will also discover exactly what a "wide range of abilities" means. You will have some students who can do whatever you ask them to do, well, in less than half the time that other students require. Plan extension activities or extra projects that will engage these students when they have finished required work. In addition, as you are planning, you may want to decide what homework activities to assign.

In planning a lesson, decide what the focus or purpose of the lesson is. It should be clearly stated, because the clearer your purpose, the easier to design a lesson that accomplishes your purpose. Some examples follow.

- The purpose of this activity is to have students use proportion to estimate the height of objects.

- The purpose of this activity is to have students use a variety of multimedia resources to explore a thematic topic in depth.

List the materials that will be needed. If you need to order any supplies or get other items, you can do so in advance.

Plan the introduction to your lesson to give students background knowledge that will help them understand the new information. Literature, songs, and pictures can build background knowledge and motivate your students.

> **Student achievement can be interpreted only in light of the quality of the program they experience.**
>
> **—National Science Education Standards**

Plan exactly what you are going to do and how you are going to do it. Walk throughout the procedure in your head. If the lesson involves following directions and/or making something, do the activity yourself before you present it to your class. This will help you identify trouble spots. It is much easier to make necessary adjustments before you present it to a group of excited fifth graders.

After you present the lesson, your students should have time to work independently on the skill you have presented. This gives them the practice necessary to learn it. You may wish to have the students work on the skill in small groups.

### TIP!

*Let your students participate in selecting some of the themes they would like to investigate.*

The final element to consider is how to assess the effectiveness of the lesson. You should use informal observations of students involved in the independent activity planned for the lesson combined with formal checks of the work. You can also spot check what students remember as part of the closing activities of the day.

Thinking through and planning each lesson is essential to your becoming the most effective teacher you can be.

# USING THEMES

Themes are big ideas that are larger than facts, concepts, and skills. Using a theme allows you to integrate several content areas into meaningful learning activities, then provides you with a framework to guide you in the design and development of your instructional program. A theme provides you with a way to make words and abstract ideas concrete, and to help your students see how ideas relate to other ideas and to their own experiences. Two examples of fifth-grade themes are *Oceans* and *China*.

As facets of the oceans theme, you and your students could read and write about oceans (language arts), make diagrams to show the mathematical portions of the earth that are covered by land and by water (math), do an experiment to find out if it is easier to float in a salty ocean or a freshwater lake (science), and create an ocean in a bottle using oil, water, and food coloring (visual arts).

As facets of the China theme, you and your class could make a picture dictionary of of new words they are learning (language arts), solve problems using the ancient Chinese puzzles called tangrams (math), practice writing Chinese characters (visual arts, language arts), and read a map of China (social studies).

Themes link concepts and skills for your students. As you present new lessons framed in the context of your thematic unit, students can easily add the new information to the knowledge they already have. It is easier for students to learn skills, because they have knowledge and experience which creates a context within which to apply the skills.

# LANGUAGE ARTS

Language arts instruction includes reading, writing, listening, thinking, and speaking. The ability to communicate ideas both orally and in writing is the focus of the language arts program in fifth grade. As you plan your language arts program, remember that you can use reading and writing for assessment purposes in all curricular areas. Although language arts processes apply across the curriculum, some specific skills to address in fifth grade are listed below.

- Summarize new information presented by others orally and write constructive comments about the format or style of delivery.

- Generate questions related to live and media presentations.

- Based on subject area information, memorize, share, or write songs, poems, speeches, choral verses, and scripts.

- Restate and respond appropriately to writing prompts.

- Know the difference between culturally specific vocabulary and vocabulary that describes dilemmas.

- Identify stereotypical vocabulary and vocabulary words, phrases, slogans, and advertisements that contain racial, cultural, sexist, and gender bias.

- Use computers, tapes, transparencies, electronic charts, and still or video cameras to store, retrieve, share, and develop ideas generated in theme projects.

- State orally and in writing a candidate's qualifications for a position.

- Develop spelling lists for writing activities from literature.

- Develop open-ended questions about literary and subject area theme activities.

- Research and respond to others' open-ended questions about literary and subject area theme activities.

- Evaluate journal entries and information in learning logs.

- Create questionnaires based on class-determined issues.

- Write and share creative encounters related to thematic materials and literature.

- Recognize, discuss, and create imitations of figurative, idiomatic language found in literature (alliteration, onomatopoeia, slang, acronyms, brand names that have become words)

- Transfer new theme unit information found in four or more reference sources into three or more graphic forms.

- Design a manipulative time line to be used for arranging, reordering, discussing, debating, and determining the correct sequence of events known prior to investigation of a topic.

- Retell and present a familiar story from the perspective of the villain rather than the usual hero or heroine.

- Develop articles and comic strips for a class newspaper based on research that brings historical information into the present.

> **We should establish classrooms where children are encouraged to take responsibility for their learning, to become independent writers, readers, thinkers, and speakers, and to take an active role in creating a more just society.**
>
> **—Michael Hartoonian**

## Recommended Core Literature Selections

The following books read aloud well in class and are appropriate for fifth grade students.

*Summer of the Monkeys* by Wilson Rawls (Bantam Books, 1992)

*Where the Red Fern Grows* by Wilson Rawls (Bantam Books, 1984)

*Sounder* by William H. Armstrong (Trophy, 1996)

*Old Yeller* by Fred Gipson (Trophy, 1990)

*Bridge to Terabithia* by Katherine Paterson (Trophy, 1996)

*From the Mixed-Up Files of Mrs. Basil E. Frankweiler* by E.L. Konigsburg (Aladdin Books, 1987)

*Ben & Me* by Robert Lawson (Little, Brown & Co. 1988)

# Reading

Two approaches to reading instruction are being used by many schools and school districts. The first is a literature-based program and the second is a traditional program.

## Literature-Based Program

In a literature-based program, reading is taught throughout the curriculum. A few selected books are read in depth. Instruction is built around activities that encourage appropriate integration of various literary forms into interdisciplinary theme units. Literature is used to reinforce and enrich skill and concept development. It is used to extend new ideas and information into different contexts. Literature is used to arouse more curiosity about something.

All of these books adjunct the core theme of American History in fifth grade. Three to four books should be selected and covered in depth. Units and study guides can be found at teacher supply stores, district resource centers, or through publishers' catalogues. You'll want to gather enough books for the entire class.

### Sample Curriculum Based on *Ben & Me* by Robert Lawson

The following activities comprise an in-depth cross-curricular study based on a core literature book.

> ### TIP!
>
> *Read books aloud to your class. Students enjoy listening to more complex stories that they might not be able to read comfortably by themselves yet.*

Introduce the book *Ben & Me* to your students by talking about the author, giving the title of the book, and explaining the type of book you'll be reading (historical fiction).

### Reading/Language

**Fact and Fiction**—You'll first want to review the terms *fact* and *fiction* with your class. Then make a poster divided into two columns using the heading *Fact or Fiction?* The students will keep track of events in the story by categorizing them in the *Fact* column or the *Fiction* column.

**Vocabulary Development**—This activity lets your students increase vocabulary and practice dictionary skills at the same time. Have the students look up the definitions of the following words found in *Ben & Me*.

| | |
|---|---|
| manuscript | severity |
| disheveled | hearthstone |
| delirious | apprentice |
| draught | rapscallion |
| decipher | disreputable |
| trousseau | hoax |
| intimacy | domicile |
| cudgel | lamented |
| despondency | bosun |
| sloop | forelock |
| innumerable | |

**Comprehension**—The following appear in *Ben & Me*. Discuss the author's use of words with your students.

"to take pen in paw"

"Waste not, want not"

"milling throng"

"stony silence"

"twitter of excitement"

"fled like snowflakes"

**Maxim**—A maxim is a concisely stated principle or rule of conduct. Keep track of the maxims found in *Ben & Me* and have students create bumper stickers for them. Post the bumper stickers around the room.

**Personification**—In this book, the author personifies a mouse by giving it human qualities. Have students list as many examples of personification as they can find in the book. Then ask "What other stories have you read that use the same literary device?" (Possible examples: *Charlotte's Web* by E.B. White (HarperCollins, 1990), *The Wind in the Willows* by Kenneth Graham (Tor Books, 1989).)

## Extended Reading

**Biographies**—Have students dress as one of the famous people listed below and give oral reports to the class.

Doctor Benjamin Franklin

John Paul Jones

Mr. Thomas Jefferson

Von Steuben

General George Washington

Lord Cornwallis

King and Queen of France

King of England

## Science

**Science Topics**—These topics are featured in *Ben & Me*. Your students can study about and explore these topics.

| | |
|---|---|
| Tides | Pulleys |
| Static Electricity | Lightning Rods |

**Conductors**—When reading chapter VII—*The Lightning Rod,* ask the question "Why was Amos safe in the glass jar?" Then begin a study on conductors.

## Research

**Research Topics**—Students work in pairs to do research on one of the following topics from *Ben & Me* and write a report to present orally to the class.

| | |
|---|---|
| Philosophical Society | Congress |
| Colonial Architecture | Versailles |
| Old Christ Church | Printing Press |
| Museum of Natural History | Franklin Stove |
| First Volunteer Fire Brigade | Colonial Period |
| Poor Richard's Almanac | Fourth of July |

## Math

**Roman Numerals**—Review Roman numerals. Then examine the table of contents in *Ben & Me*. Give your students craft sticks and glue to make individual sets of the numerals in the table of contents.

## Geography

**Map Reading**—Have students locate the following places mentioned in the story and mark them on a class map. As an extension activity, students can make their own passports and record all the countries they've visited through literature.

| | |
|---|---|
| Philadelphia | Valley Forge |
| Schuylkill River | Russia |
| England | Denmark |
| Massachusetts | Sweden |
| Virginia | Spain |
| Mount Vernon | Atlantic Ocean |
| France | Italy |
| Paris | |

> [A student] wants to feel that the instructor is not simply passing on dead knowledge in the form that it was passed on to him, but that he has assimilated it and has read his own experience into it, so that it has come to mean more to him than almost anything in the world.
>
> —Randolph Bourne, <u>Youth and Life</u>, 1913

### Other Books by Robert Lawson

*Captain Kidd's Cat*
(Little, Brown, 1984)

*The Fabulous Flight*
(Little, Brown, 1984)

*Rabbit Hill*
(Puffin Books, 1977)

*Mr. Revere and I*
(Little, Brown, 1988)

### Illustrated by Robert Lawson

*Mr. Popper's Penguins*
by Richard and Florence Atwater (Little, Brown, 1992)

*The Story of Ferdinand*
by Munro Leaf (Puffin Books, 1993)

### History

Have students research the following facets of history mentioned in *Ben & Me.*

- Relations between American Colonies and Mother Country England
- King and Parliament
- Stamp Taxes
- Revolutionary War
- Aid from France
- Declaration of Independence
- French Revolution

### Music

**Yankee Doodle**—The song "Yankee Doodle" is featured in the book. Sing the song with the class. Then challenge the students to write new verses for the song.

**Orchestra**—An orchestra is featured in the book. Begin a study on the orchestra.

### Multicultural Education

**Foreign Language**—As Ben visits France in the story, introduce some basic French words. The numbers from 1–10 are listed below.

| | |
|---|---|
| 1. un | 6. six |
| 2. deux | 7. sept |
| 3. trois | 8. huit |
| 4. quatre | 9. neuf |
| 5. cinq | 10. dix |

## A Reading Workshop

Set aside time each day for a reading workshop where skills are taught using literature. These stages should

**TIP!**

*Videotape or take photographs of projects to share ideas with parents at Open House and with next year's class.*

be included in each reading workshop.

### Oral Reading

Read a good book, poem, folktale, or short story to your students.

### Mini-Lessons

Use the book or story you have read to teach a skill such as identifying metaphors or distinguishing between fact and opinion. After students listen to the story, reread it focusing on the skill.

### Personal Reading

Students devote this time to reading. Depending on your schedule and your students' abilities, you will want this period to last 10–30 minutes. The room should be quiet and the students encouraged to read books at their ability level. You should also read during this time so the students see you modeling good reading habits.

time. Establish a reading corner in the room for students to do this free reading since most fifth graders enjoy moving around and being able to leave their desks. Providing areas for free movement helps eliminate possible discipline problems

## Classroom Library

Provide a classroom library that is an inviting and comfortable place. Arrange the books by category and color-code them so your students can easily locate titles. You may wish to furnish the library area with pillows and bean bag chairs.

## Author Study

Having your students study several works of literature by the same author will lead to them having favorite authors that they will choose to read over and over again. Each time students read two or more books by the same author, have them do an author study. You may choose to use the form found on page 31.

## Poetry

Poetry is the language of the imagination expressed rhythmically. Exposing your student to different kinds of poetry serves many purposes. Here are some of the benefits.

- Poetry introduces students to good literature.

- It helps students appreciate rhythm, meter, and rhyme.

- Poetry motivates students in writing and other creative activities.

- It helps students learn to express many moods.

- Poetry helps them learn to identify the following literary techniques:

  **Alliteration**—repetition of the same initial consonant sounds (softly, swirling snow)

*Response Time*

Give opportunities for the students to respond to the books they've read. Students may, for example, act out a scene from the book, create a new ending to the story, or put on a puppet show about the book.

*Conferences*

Meet with several students each day to give encouragement and assistance, to help students set reading goals, and to listen to students read aloud. Conferences can be with individual students or small groups of students. Use the Conference Record Sheet on page 32 to track student progress.

*Sharing*

End each workshop with a sharing session. Allow the students to share their books and responses with the class. Each student will not have a chance to share every day. Make a schedule so that everyone has a turn to share at least once a week.

*Assessment*

Keep a log for each student. Write down what types of books the student is reading, how he or she is progressing, and areas of strengths and weaknesses.

## Free Reading

Encourage students to keep a reading book in their desks so that they can read whenever their classroom work is completed and they have extra

> **Reading is to the mind what exercise is to the body.**
> —**Sir Richard Steele**

## Literature Appreciation

*Cinderella or The Little Glass Slipper* by Charles Perrault (Henry Z. Walck, Inc., 1970) This is the original French version translated into English.

*Cinderella: and other tales from Perrault* illustrated by Michael Hague (Holt & Co., 1989) This is a traditional retelling with beautiful drawings.

*The Brocaded Slipper and Other Vietnamese Tales* by Lynette Dyer Vuong (Trophy, 1992)

*Moss Gown* by William H. Hooks (Clarion, 1990) This is a traditional Southern version.

*The Egyptian Cinderella* by Shirley Climo (Crowell Jr. Books, 1989) This version takes place in ancient Egypt.

*Mufaro's Beautiful Daughters* by John Steptoe (Lothrop, Lee & Shepard Books, 1987) This version is from Africa.

*Prince Cinders* by Babette Cole (Sandcastle Books, 1992) This is a modern version with a twist.

*Princess Furball* by Charlotte Huck (Greenwillow, 1989) This is a version from England.

*Yeh-Shen: A Cinderella Story from China* by Ai-Ling Louie (Philomel Books, 1990)

**Metaphor**—implied comparison of two different things that have something in common (His arms were iron bands.)

**Simile**—stated comparison of two unlike things using the words *like* or *as.* (Her eyes were like stars.)

**Hyperbole**—an exaggerated statement (He is as strong as an ox.)

**Personification**—giving life to a non-living subject

**Onomatopoeia**—a word that sounds like what you are describing (buzz)

## Literature Appreciation

Another type of literature appreciation can be explored by reading the same story in many different versions. The story of Cinderella has been told in many d i f f e r e n t countries. Use this list to help locate various versions to read to the class.

After reading several versions, have students compare and contrast cultures, geographic locations, and local customs. Have students identify which versions they enjoyed the most and why.

## Traditional Program

In a traditional program, reading is taught as an isolated skill. Basal readers with workbooks and accompanying worksheets that reinforce vocabulary and comprehension skills are used. End-of-book tests are taken and pre-packaged reading labs are used to reinforce skills. Students are often motivated to read by contests and by recording their progress on charts. Book reports are usually required.

### *Reading Comprehension*

Having students answer questions about a reading assignment is one way to display your students' understanding. Here are some sample questions for fiction books:

1. How can you tell where the story took place?

2. What gave you clues as to when the story took place?

3. Is the main character like or unlike anyone you know? In what ways?

4. Would you choose the main character to be your friend? Why or why not?

5. How did the characters get along with one another?

6. What problems did the characters have to overcome?

7. What part of the story could not happen in real life? Why? (This is for a fantasy story.)

8. Who told the story? How do you know?

**TIP!**

*At the end of the year, let the students make a mural featuring their favorite books and authors.*

Here are some questions for non-fiction books:

1. What new fact(s) did you learn from this book?

2. How many new vocabulary words did you learn and what were they?

3. Did the book hold your interest? Why or why not?

### Book Reports

It will help if you establish a required book report assignment list at the beginning of the school year. This list may be given to the student, the parent(s), and posted in the classroom. Include this information on the list: the date assigned, the due date, and the specific type of book to be read. Fifth graders read from the following categories: fantasy, mystery, science fiction, biography, realistic fiction, historical fiction, as well as several free-choice selections. You'll want to include directions and general guidelines. The students should three-hole punch their assignment lists and keep them in their notebooks under "language arts" or "book reports". (This helps students with organizational skills, which is a consistent theme in fifth grade.) Here is one example of directions you might use: *Each month you will be assigned a book report assignment for a specific type of book. Points for neatness and creativity will be included in your grade. You will also write a summary of your book in class and log your book onto your book list. Some months you will be given free choice which means that you select any type of book to read. It should be a book that you have not read before. Check with your teacher if you are unsure of your choice of book. Books should be around 150 pages long.*

The reading log can be written in class. This is a one-page summary of the book used to check comprehension and writing skills. Because the students are assigned a specific type of book to read each month, the summary writing can be modeled on the board as a whole class lesson before the individual summaries are attempted. Vary the opening statements according to the type of book. An example of this would be: *The Clue in the Attic is a mystery.; James and the Giant Peach is an adventure story.* [James and the Giant Peach by Roald Dahl (Riffin, 1988)] By keeping the opening statement simple the student is able to support one main idea with three supporting sentences. The three supporting sentences should be examples that illustrate the main idea. The final sentence is the closing statement that wraps up the main idea by restating it. Here are some examples of closing sentences: *All of these clues helped solve the mystery.; These events are examples of the adventures James had in the book.* Since fifth graders tend to retell the entire story, you'll want to ask for concise summaries that don't exceed the amount of space given for the assignment.

### Types of Book Reports

Here is a list of book report ideas. Offer the students a choice each month from two or three different ideas. This helps to make sure that a student doesn't do the same type of project each time. Students may want to suggest their own ideas.

**Time Line**—Students list important events in a person's life or in the story. Included are dates and illustrations. (This is especially suitable for historical fiction and biographies.)

**Dioramas**—Students make a three-dimensional display of a scene from the book. (A shoebox may be used.)

> **To read without reflecting is like eating without digesting.**
> —Edmund Burke

**Story Map**—Students chart a story visually by drawing a map that illustrates the character's travels. A compass rose is included.

**Time Capsule**—Students make a time capsule and fill it with items from the story. If some items are not available, pictures from magazines or student-drawn illustrations can be placed in the capsule.

**Model**—Students make a model of an item or event from the book using clay, wood, Legos®, or any other appropriate media.

**Song**—Students create a song about the book and write it or tape it for the class to hear.

**Poster**—Students make a poster advertising the book.

**Book Cover**—Students design a new illustration for the cover of the book.

**Mobile**—Students design a mobile using a wire clothes hanger. The characters, setting, and events from the book may all be displayed.

**Oral Book Reports**—These work well for biographies. Students can dress up as the person featured in the biography and give an oral presentation to the class. Arrange for the students to be able to change their clothes before their presentations. Schedule 4–5 presenters for each day randomly by pulling their names out of a can. Allow students to have notes on index cards to refer to if needed during their presentations. It also helps to put a time limit on these presentations. Three to five minutes is suitable for fifth grade. Here are some guidelines that help the students organize their facts and summarize the material they've read.

1. Introduce the famous person to the class by name, "I am . . . "

2. Tell the class interesting facts about the famous person.

3. On the class map, show where the person lived.

4. Tell the class when the person lived or if the person is still living.

5. Explain why you enjoyed learning about this person.

> ### TIP!
>
> *Let the students design awards for books they have read using categories such as best illustrations, funniest book, best mystery, best science fiction book, etc.*

### Storyboards

Another way to check comprehension is to assign a storyboard or time line of the book. Storyboards include the setting, characters, and main events from the story. Large index cards work well for this assignment and can be taped together for an informative bulletin board display. Remind students to enhance their pictures with color. Adding machine tape works well for time lines. Give each student a strip of tape to write out and illustrate the story chronologically. These make good partner assignments.

### Grammar

Display sentences containing grammatical errors as students enter the classroom each morning. Have students write the sentence correctly in a journal each day. Go over the sentences with the class.

### Venn Diagrams

Use Venn Diagrams to compare and contrast different books. Start with two circles, one representing each book. The intersecting parts share common themes. Then work up to three circles with intersecting sections between two circles and all three circles.

### Vocabulary

Vocabulary lists can be generated from reading assignments. Have students define each word, identify the sentence from the book where the word is used, and identify the part of speech. This helps to build vocabularies, strengthen dictionary skills, and helps with grammar.

### Drama

Role playing or dramatizing are effective ways to check comprehension in fifth grade since students have a natural enjoyment of talking and being on stage. Divide the class into small groups of three to four to dramatize a chapter of a book, a theme from a poem, or to show a new ending for a story. Some productions only require a limited amount of preparation time and can be completed in class on the day it is assigned. Other productions require more elaborate preparation time. Costumes and props from home can enhance these performances. Set a time limit for the performances and tell students that inappropriate language or violence is not allowed. You may want to videotape these skits to view in class.

### Reports

Student-oriented topics of interest for short research assignments also provide practice in reading comprehension. Having students present the reports orally in front of the class strengthens their speaking skills. Here are some tips to share and discuss.

• Practice saying your report out loud before presenting it to the class.

> **Excite new ways of seeing, feeling and being, in order to preserve the innate creative potential of every one of us.**
>
> **—Ann Wiseman: Making Things**

• Project your voice to the back of the room.

• Make eye contact with members of your audience.

• Speak slowly.

• Use good posture.

Before outlining and discussing the tips, demonstrate their opposites to the class. Have students identify the ineffective aspects of your demonstration. Information students discover on their own is better learned.

## Oral Reading

Students enjoy being read to by the teacher and each other. Every day, spend some time reading aloud to your class. Shared oral reading can be used to introduce or support themes or new activities, provide background information, practice reading strategies, or just share the pleasure of reading. You could read a book you have multiple copies of and have students follow along with you in their copies or choose a favorite children's novel and read a chapter a day every day until you have finished it. This allows your students to experience literature that they may not be able to read on their own. Students will also enjoy taking turns reading aloud to the class. Any assigned class reading can be done in the round-robin style by having each student take a turn reading an assigned number of paragraphs or pages. Give students the right to pass when they are not in the mood to read aloud. Fifth graders enjoy chapter books, poetry, and American folklore, and classics.

**23**

## Independent Reading

### D.E.A.R. Time

D.E.A.R. time means Drop Everything and Read time. Many schools recommend or require D.E.A.R. time. If yours doesn't, you may wish to implement it in your classroom. During this time, the only activity going on in your room is reading. Your students read, classroom visitors read, and you read.

### Sustained Silent Reading

Sustained Silent Reading is a time that students devote to reading. Depending on your schedule and your students' abilities, you will want this period to last 15–45 minutes. The room should be quiet and the students encouraged to read books at their ability levels for the duration of the period.

## Library Visits

Visits to the library give students an opportunity to select books to read. Arrange these visits with your school librarian and, if possible, the public librarian, and ask if they could help sharpen and reinforce the research skills your students are learning at school. Explore the Dewey Decimal system and show students how to locate a book using the library's computer. By giving the librarian a copy of your book report schedule, selected books from your category of choice can be on display and when special research projects are being worked on, those books can be available. Encourage your students to have their own public library cards. You will want to inquire about special privileges at a public library that you as a teacher may be entitled to, such as free video rental for classroom use.

## Writing

Writing is an essential part of language arts learning. Research has proven that writing improves reading.

### TIP!

*Let your students see you reading often. This gives the message that reading is important.*

## The Writing Process

Writing is a process which includes five stages. Your students will need a great deal of practice in all phases of the writing process in order to become effective writers. An explanation of the steps of the writing process follow.

**Prewriting**—During this stage, students generate writing ideas and decide who the audience will be. Methods such as brainstorming, debating, mapping, and fantasizing are used.

**Drafting**—At this stage, students organize their thoughts and a rough draft is created from an idea from the prewriting stage. Students do not need to be concerned with spelling and punctuation at this time.

**Revising**—This stage allows students to decide on ways to make their writing better by reading what they have written and deciding which parts need more detail, which words and phrases are overused, and if enough descriptive words and powerful action words are included. The students may get feedback from you or their peers. See page 33 for a form that evaluators may fill out.

**Proofreading**—This is the time to correct spelling, syntax, and mechanical errors. At this time students recopy the revised draft neatly. You may want to have partners use the form found on page 34 to help each other proofread.

**Publishing**—This stage gives students an opportunity to share their own writing and enjoy the creative work of others. Here are some publishing ideas:

*Individual Books*—Students make their final drafts into books and then illustrate their work. The books may be shaped, covered with contact paper or fabric, or covered with a three-ring binder.

*Reading*—Hold a reading and invite other classes from your school. Let students read aloud a favorite piece of writing.

*Video Stories*—Videotape the students reading a favorite story and let the students take the video home on a rotating basis to share with their families.

*Act It Out!*—Have groups of students perform their stories as plays for the entire class.

## Writing Workshop

One way to manage a writing program in your classroom is by having an ongoing writing workshop. Writing workshops give your students a great deal of practice in all phases of the writing process. A great advantage of a writing workshop is that the students can work at their own paces and they sharpen their skills over the year. They look forward to writing time when they can be creative, productive, and challenged all at the same time. You will be proud of the progress your students make.

It is extremely helpful to have a parent volunteer assist with the Workshop. If you have a computer in your classroom, or a volunteer who will do word processing for you, student books can be electronically published. Electronic publishing adds an exciting touch to the process for your students.

## Mini-Lessons

You will present mini-lessons during writing workshops. These lessons should only last five to ten minutes and should focus on a specific topic. Possible topics include specific types of writing such as narratives, verse, friendly letters, advertisements, oral histories, autobiographical and biographical sketches, the purpose and audience for each type of writing, and specific proofreading skills. As you review the students' works-in-progress, you will identify areas you want your students to strengthen. Your students may also suggest topics to you.

After presenting a mini-lesson, review the status of the class. Ask each student, "What will you be working on?" The student might reply, "I'm rewriting my story, or I'm editing my draft." The status check should only take two to three minutes. Based on the responses you receive, you know who needs help right away.

## Writing Conferences

Meeting individually with students can help them improve their writing. Conferences give students an opportunity to evaluate their own writing and receive feedback. During the writing conference, follow these guidelines.

- Have the student read his or her writing to you.

- Ask the student to tell you what part needs more work.

- Have the student tell you what part he or she is most pleased with.

- Provide feedback and suggest ways to improve the writing.

- Address formal and informal assessments of student progress and skill needs.

- Discuss which items will be further developed, edited, and published.

- Make notes about the student's progress.

Students may also hold student-student conferences in addition to the teacher-student conferences. Use the conference record on page 32 to track student progress.

> **The art of teaching, then, lies in helping students discover how good listeners, speakers, readers, and writers accomplish their ends in communicating with others.**
>
> —**Effective Instruction in English-Language Arts**

## Assessment

Here are some ways to evaluate student writing.

**Portfolios**—Use portfolios to accurately measure your students' development and achievement. A writing portfolio consists of writing samples collected over a period of time and includes both teacher-selected and student-selected samples. It also includes written observations made by the teacher and self-evaluations made by the student. Portfolios are beneficial because:

- The teacher can see student growth.

- The teacher can plan lessons based on the students' needs.

- Students share the responsibility of evaluating their work.

- Parents can see student growth.

- Administrators can see what is going on in the classroom.

**Writing Checklist**—Make a checklist by listing the writing skills you have taught across the top of a sheet of graphing paper. Then list the students' names down the left side. Keep track of progress by checking off when a student incorporates a particular skill into his or her writing.

**Rubrics**—A rubric is a scoring guide which lists the criteria for each score. Rubrics may be based on various scales, which may have up to nine points. Try to avoid using rubrics with only four points as

> **TIP!**
>
> *Mini-lessons are short and sweet...use five minutes to present information and use five minutes for guided practice.*

this too closely relates to the common grading scale of A to F. Each rubric should be tailored to the specific writing task. The rubrics should be clearly established before the rough draft stage so that the student knows what will be evaluated. A sample rubric follows for an assignment in which students were asked to describe a restaurant that they remember vividly. It could be the best, worst, or most unusual. The description should include all five senses.

**Score 9–8**—This score applies to papers with excellent organization, content, and use of language and mechanics. An 8 paper is a thinner version of a 9 paper. Most or all of the following are done well:

- developed a good introduction

- maintained an appropriate point of view

- used descriptive vocabulary

- did not shift in tense or person

- organized ideas effectively and provided an introduction, closure, and an orderly progression from one idea to another

- used at least three of the five senses

**Score 7**—This score applies to papers that have most of the criteria for the 9–8 paper, but lack some organization and have more language and mechanical problems.

**Score 6–4**—This score applies to papers that maintain the general idea of the assignment, but are weak in content. These characteristics are noticeable:

- introduction is weak

- has shifts in tense and person

- minimally organized

- has serious errors in mechanics, usage, and sentence structure

- uses at least one of the five senses

Score 3–2—This score applies to papers that make no attempt to address the topic. These characteristics are noticed:

- no organization

- constantly shifts in tense and person

- contains many sentence errors

- serious errors in English making it difficult for a reader to follow

- none of the five senses is mentioned

Score 1—This score applies to papers that have nothing to do with the topic and no effort is made.

# Writing Across the Curriculum

Writing is ideal for all areas of the curriculum. Here are a few tried and true activities that will keep your students motivated.

## Literature

New Ending—Write a new ending for a story.

Sequel—Write an outline for a sequel to a story.

Diary—Pretend to be one of the main characters from a story and write a page in his or her diary.

Dear Characters—Write a letter to your favorite characters from a story and tell why you enjoy them.

## Art

"How-To"—Write the directions for completing an art project. The directions should be written for someone who has never done the project. For example, how to weave a placemat or how to fold a piece of paper into a ball. Then give the directions to classmates to see if they can follow them.

## Science

Explain It—Write an explanation about a science concept such as *For every action there is an equal and opposite reaction.*

## Math

Word Problems—Create story problems for others to solve.

## Social Studies

Pen Pals—Write to other fifth-grade classes at other schools.

First, find the name of some other schools and write to the principals. Ask them to forward your request for pen pals to the fifth-grade teachers.

Once you've established contact, your students can write letters. Your students will look forward to receiving mail from their new friends. Once the letters start arriving, post a map in the classroom and place stickers where the pen pals live.

Business Letters—Write business letters to state tourism departments requesting information to use in their state reports.

> **Never discourage anyone...who continually makes progress, no matter how slow.**
> —Plato

**27**

**Me Book**—This is an alphabetical and creative autobiography in which each letter of the alphabet is represented on a separate page. This should be a long-term assignment. Each page should include one sentence about the student using the following sentence starters:

*All about the widely acclaimed ...*
*Beyond belief, the best book I ever read is ...*
*Creatively talented when ...*
*Dignified and darling*
*during ...*
*Enjoys eating ...*
*Fabulous friends include ...*
*Grand and glorious when ...*
*Highly handsome feature*
*is ...*
*Inventions I intend to invent*
*are ...*
*Jumping into a job as ...*
*The kindest, kingly act I've done was ...*
*Loveable and likeable when ...*
*The most magnificent moment was when ...*
*Noted for nervousness when ...*
*Once, the one and only ...*
*Perfectly pleased when ...*

*Quick and quiet when ...*
*Radiant, radical, and renowned for ...*
*Superb at the sport of ...*
*Truly favorite toy is ...*
*Universally known for ...*
*Very concerned about ...*
*Wonderful when ...*
*Extra special places I've visited*
*are ...*
*You know I'd like to go to ...*
*Zany zoo animal for a pet would*
*be ...*

**TIP!**

*Feature a student each week to be Author of the Week. Display a picture and biography of the student and selected writing samples.*

You'll want to spend time going over the instructions and expectations for this assignment. Discuss time management skills and strategies for completing the assignment. Explain how to organize the work so that a small amount of time is spend each day working on the report rather than waiting until the last minute. Encourage students with access to a word processor to use their computers for the report.

**It's a [darn] poor mind that can think of only one way to spell a word!**

**—Revised from Andrew Jackson, quoted in an advertisement (1982)**

## Using Journals

Use journals in your classroom to allow students to experiment with writing styles, explore their feelings, and practice writing in a risk-free setting. These are some ways that journals can be used.

**Daily Writing**—Have students use spiral-bound or loose-leaf notebooks for a journal to write in each day. Schedule a specific time for writing in this journal. Provide topics or let the students choose their own topics. Rather than writing grades or making corrections in this journal, respond through written comments such as, "Interesting, I'd like to hear more about it!" The students will look forward to reading your comments.

**Learning Logs**—Your students can use journals to record what they are learning in content areas.

**Personal Journals**—Your students can write about anything they want to in these journals. Respect the students' privacy with these journals since they might be writing about something very personal. Tell the students that you will not read these journals unless they want to share them with you. If the students know that their privacy will be respected, they will more likely write about their true feelings.

**Dialogue Journals**—These journals may be used to record dialogue between you and your students. You can communicate about concerns, schoolwork, or home activities.

## Spelling

There are different ways to approach spelling instruction in your fifth-grade classroom. You may have to use a program required by your school. If you have a choice, you might choose the approach that works best for your students. Here are a few options.

**Traditional Approach**—With this approach, there are spelling books with a designated number of words for each week. The words are usually grouped in some way such as by word families. All students have the same list. With this method, you may want to add additional bonus or challenge words from other curriculum areas to the weekly list. The students are usually given a formal test each Friday.

These are typical assignments with a traditional program.

1. Write the words in alphabetical order.

2. Write the definitions for each word using a dictionary.

3. Write complete sentences using the words.

4. Write a synonym for each word.

5. Write an antonym for each word.

6. Create a crossword puzzle using the words.

7. Create a word search puzzle using the words.

**Integrated Spelling**—This method requires a list of words that is relevant to what the students are studying in school rather than a designated list. It can be very motivating to students to select the words they will learn to spell. You would test regularly to assess their knowledge of the spelling of those words.

**Individualized Spelling**—With this approach, the students identify words from their own writings that they need to learn to spell. Each student creates his or her own list. Once the students can show in their daily writing that they can spell a word from the list, they can cross it off. New words are constantly being added to the list.

# Personal Dictionaries

Have students keep an alphabetical list of words that they misspell or need help spelling in a notebook o journal. Students should first refer to this list whenever they need the spelling of a word. Here is a list o some commonly misspelled words. You may want to post them in the classroom for students to refer to

| | | | | | |
|---|---|---|---|---|---|
| about | cough | hear | o'clock | several | truly |
| advise | could | heard | off | since | two |
| again | couldn't | height | often | something | until |
| against | country | here | once | sometime | used |
| already | cousin | hospital | party | soon | usually |
| although | dairy | hour | peace | straight | vacation |
| always | dear | house | people | study | vegetable |
| among | decorate | instead | piece | suppose | very |
| aunt | describe | interest | played | sure | wear |
| awhile | didn't | knew | please | surely | weather |
| balloon | doctor | know | practice | surprise | weigh |
| because | early | letter | pretty | surround | were |
| been | enough | little | principle | teacher | we're |
| before | every | loose | quarter | terrible | when |
| believe | everybody | lose | quiet | their | where |
| birthday | except | loving | quite | there | which |
| bought | favorite | making | raise | they | white |
| built | fierce | many | receive | though | whole |
| business | first | maybe | received | thought | woman |
| busy | football | minute | remember | tired | women |
| buy | forty | morning | right | together | would |
| calendar | fourth | mother | rough | tomorrow | write |
| chocolate | friend | muscle | route | tonight | wrote |
| choose | fuel | neither | said | too | yesterday |
| close | guard | nice | says | toys | you |
| color | guess | niece | school | train | your |
| coming | haven't | none | separate | trouble | you're |

Name _____

# Author Study

Author's Name _____

These are the titles of the books I read:

_____

_____

_____

_____

This is what I like about this author's writing: _____

_____

_____

_____

_____

If I could meet this author, this is what I would tell him or her: _____

_____

_____

_____

_____

_____

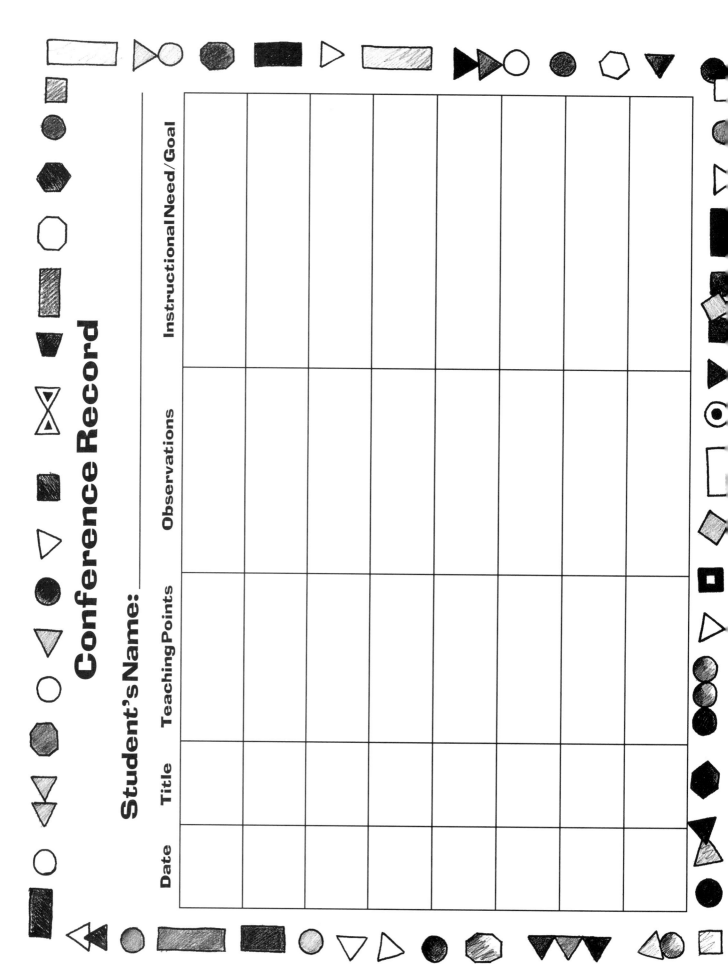

# Conference Record

**Student's Name:** _____

| Date | Title | Teaching Points | Observations | Instructional Need/Goal |
|---|---|---|---|---|
| | | | | |
| | | | | |
| | | | | |
| | | | | |
| | | | | |

# Revision Form

Let a classmate read your writing. Then have him or her fill out this form.

Author's Name _____

Title of Writing _____

Evaluator's Name _____

Is the writing easy to understand? _____

Tell about an interesting part. _____

_____

What would you like to know more about? _____

_____

_____

What was your favorite part? Tell why. _____

_____

_____

List any overused words or phrases. _____

_____

Do you have any suggestions to make it more interesting? _____

_____

_____

# Proofreading Form

Let a classmate proofread your work. Then have him or her fill out this form and review your writing with you.

Author's Name _____

Title of Writing _____

Proofreader's Name _____

Does each sentence begin with a capital letter? _____

Does each sentence end with correct punctuation? _____

Is each word spelled correctly? _____

Is each sentence a complete thought? _____

Is the handwriting neat? _____

Do you have any suggestions? _____

_____

_____

_____

_____

_____

# MATHEMATICS

The focus of math instruction in fifth grade is a deep understanding of concepts. In fifth grade, students have a wide range of abilities. As you develop your math program, try to focus on math as a part of your students' everyday lives. Try to incorporate math in any possible situation. If three students are absent , ask students "What fraction of the class is here today?" or "What percentage of the class is absent?" Any and all questions that stimulate discussion and problem solving are advantageous. You may choose to give a pre-test at the beginning of the school year to pinpoint areas of strength or weakness. Although math can be applied to all areas of the curriculum, some specific skills to address in fifth grade are listed below.

- Apply number concepts to real problem situations.

- Read, write, order, use numbers, and express their place values.

- Develop operation concepts of whole numbers and money.

- Use estimation and mental computation strategies to find sums, differences, products, and quotients.

- Investigate the relationships of decimals as parts to a whole.

- Investigate and express the place value of decimals through thousandths.

- Analyze, compare, order, and round decimals.

- Develop operation concepts of decimals.

- Use estimation and mental computation strategies to find sums, differences, products, or quotients of decimals, money, or fractions.

- Select and use appropriate method of computing.

- Explore relationships between fractions and decimals.

- Analyze and find equivalent fractions.

- Analyze and simplify fractions.

- Explore relationships between mixed numbers and improper fractions.

- Express the relationship of one number to another as a ratio.

- Analyze whether two simple rations are proportional.

- Make reasonable conclusions about situations represented by mathematical sentences.

- Express lines, points, rays, and line segments and relate them to shapes in the environment.

- Determine whether two geometric shapes are similar.

> **We must go beyond what we were taught and teach how we wish we had been taught. We must bring to life a vision of what a mathematics classroom should be . . .**
>
> **—Miriam A. Leiva, Curriculum and Evaluation Standards for School Mathematics, Addenda Series**

- Express congruent shapes, angles, and line segments.

- Express the properties of a cone, cube, cylinder, sphere, prism, and pyramid.

- Express the properties of parallel, perpendicular, and intersecting lines.

- Classify square, rectangle, rhombus, parallelogram, and trapezoid by shape.

- Analyze and classify right, acute, and obtuse angles.

- Analyze and classify a triangle by its angles or sides.

- Estimate and verify the perimeters of polygons.

- Estimate and verify the areas of plane shapes.

- Estimate and measure weight, length, volume, and capacity in metric and customary units.

- Select the most appropriate unit to measure.

- Estimate and read temperatures in Celsius and Fahrenheit.

- Analyze, extend, and create complex number patterns.

- Analyze and graph an ordered pair for a specific point on a number plane.

- Analyze, extend, and create lists of ordered pairs.

- Express additional ordered pairs when discovering a function rule.

- Express the function rule when given ordered pairs.

- Collect, organize, display, interpret, and analyze data in bar, line, and circle graphs, tables, and charts.

- Predict outcomes and record results of simple probability experiments.

- Use simple tables or diagrams to represent possible outcomes of an experiment.

- Express the operation symbol which makes a number sentence true.

- Show an understanding of the commutative, associative, and distributive properties by expressing the missing number in a number sentence.

- Write a mathematical expression for a phrase or sentence.

- Express a number represented by "$n$" in an equation.

- Use and explain simple formulas.

- Analyze and substitute a value for a variable, and simplify.

## Problem Solving

Problem solving is an important focus of the mathematics curriculum. In true problem solving, the student is given an unfamiliar situation for which no immediate path to the answer is apparent. Problem solving is the process by which the student resolves the unfamiliar situation. This is different from traditional word problems in which a student solves a problem, but doesn't actually problem-solve. Problem solving is a skill that will benefit students throughout their entire lives. Here are some ways that you can teach your students to become successful problem solvers.

- Problem solving requires students to think. Encourage them to express their thoughts about a problem. Don't dismiss a response that seems unusual, but instead analyze why that response was given.

- Emphasize the *solution*, rather than the *answer*. The answer is merely a part of the solution.

The chart that follows lists the four steps to problem solving success.

## Steps to Problem Solving

**Think**—Carefully examine the problem to find out what is happening. Identify the facts and the question(s). Visualize the situation. Look at the data and decide what's missing. Then estimate your answer.

**Plan**—Fit the facts together and decide how to find the answer. Select a strategy (charts, tables, graphs, diagrams) to solve the problem and choose the appropriate operations.

**Solve**—Use computational, algebraic, and geometric skills to solve the problem.

**Look Back**—Check your answer for accuracy. Check it for reasonability. Make sure your solution answers the question. If it doesn't, figure out what went wrong.

Here are some problem-solving strategies that will help your students investigate and understand math content.

- Decide whether a problem contains too little, too much, or enough information.

- Use a table to solve problems.

- Make and use drawings to solve problems.

- Solve problems using a guess and check method.

- Solve a problem with many steps by solving one step at a time.

- Use logical thinking to solve problems.

- Solve problems using a model.

### Problem Solving Activities

**Situational Problem Solving**—Have the students plan a week's vacation for a family of five. Provide the students with a budget and have them research such expenses as transportation, lodging, meals, souvenirs, and admissions to places of interest.

**Making and Using Tables**—Have the students solve problems using tables. Give situations such as *Melissa practiced piano 5 minutes a day for a week. She then doubled her practice time each week for 4 more weeks. How many minutes was she practicing after the 4 weeks.* (80 minutes)

**Guess and Test**—Give students lots of practice with this strategy. Remind them to begin with a reasonable first guess, but not to be concerned if the guess doesn't work. An incorrect guess often helps the students make a better guess. Give problems such as *Dylan is twice as old as Jake. Together their ages add up to 21. How old is Jake?* (7)

**Finding Another Way**—Remind students that sometimes a problem can be solved in more than one way. Challenge students to find more than one way to find the solution to problems such as *Find the sum of these numbers: 3+7+9+10+5+8=* (Students should show different ways to find the answer 42.)

**Using a Drawing**—Tell students that to understand a problem, sometimes it helps to make a drawing. Have students draw pictures to solve problems such as *The bus stop is 875 feet to the right of Holly's house. Jasmine lives 945 feet to the right of Holly. Jack lives 250 feet to the left of the bus stop. How far does Jack live from Jasmine?* (320 feet)

## Reasoning

Reasoning activities are essential to critical thinking in math. Here are some ideas to help you get started.

### Estimation

Estimation is a valuable math skill that helps students with logical thinking and problem solving. You may want to try these ideas.

**Estimation Jar**—Start with a large, plastic jar with a screw on lid, and completely fill it with the same items such as table tennis balls, marbles, walnuts, or marshmallows. Write how many of the items are in the jar and tape the answer to the inside of the lid. Place the jar on a table with a blank poster on which students will record their estimates. Give students a week to guess how many

> **A richer mathematics program is also supported by an explosion of new mathematical knowledge—more mathematics has been created in this century than in all our previous history.**
>
> —Miriam A. Leiva, <u>Curriculum and Evaluation Standards for School Mathematics, Addenda Series</u>

items are in the jar, write their estimate on a self-stick note, and post it on the estimation poster. At the end of the week announce whose estimate was the closest. Let that student suggest what could go into the estimation jar the following week. As you do this week after week, you'll notice your students' estimation skills greatly improve.

**Pot of Gold**—Try this as a seasonal idea for St. Patrick's Day. Spray dried lima beans with gold paint to use as leprechaun's gold and place the beans in the estimation jar. Paint the beans in a well-ventilated area when students aren't present. Have students write their guesses on green shamrocks.

**Wrapping Paper**—Wrapping paper can be used for an interesting estimation challenge. Find paper with dots or stars. Then have students estimate how many dots or stars are on a sheet.

## Logical Thinking

Students need lots of practice making logical conclusions about mathematical situations. Here are a few suggestions.

**Who Am I?**—During a study of place value, give such problems as *My tens digit is 3 times my ones digit. My hundreds digit is my tens digit plus 2. My ones digit is 2.* (862)

**Choosing Coins**—While studying money, pose such questions as *Would you rather have a pound of quarters or 3 pounds of nickels?* (1 pound of quarters is worth more.) or *I have nickels, dimes, and quarters in my pocket. One half of the coins are dimes. One fourth of the coins are nickels. I have 3 quarters. How many coins do I have?* (12 coins)

## Mental Math

The more practice students have with mental math, the more successful they will be. Start with simple problems and increase difficulty as your students skill levels improve.

**Basic Facts**—Give students problems such as *18–3+6+1–5=* (17) or *6+6–2+8–10=* (8)

**Multiplying Two Digits**—Help your students mentally multiply two-digit numbers by one-digit numbers by teaching them to first find the product of the ones, then find the product of the tens, and then add the products in their heads.

Example: 4 x 65 =

**Step 1**—4 x 5 = 20

**Step 2**—4 x 60 = 240

**Step 3**—20 + 240 = 260

**Division Patterns**—Assign such problems as *Begin with 200. Divide by 4. Add 30. Divide by 8. Subtract 3. Multiply by 6. Add 40. What's the answer?* (82) Have students create their own problems for classmates to solve.

## Manipulatives

Hands-on activities with manipulatives keep students actively involved in their learning. Manipulatives may be used to introduce, reinforce, and extend any math concept. Here are a few ways to use manipulatives in your math program.

**Measurement**—Provide each student with a set of red, green, and yellow squares cut out of construction paper. Tell students that the red squares represent inches, the green squares represent feet, and the yellow squares represent yards. Write the following on the chalkboard:

12 inches (12 red) = 1 foot (1 green)

3 feet (3 green) = 1 yard (1 blue)

Give students addition and subtraction problems to solve. Have them use the squares to check their answers. Example: *3 ft. 6 in. + 1 ft. 7 in.= (5 ft. 1 in.)* Have them create new problems for their classmates.

**Money**—Provide each student with a supply of play money including one-dollar, five-dollar, ten-dollar, twenty-dollar, fifty-dollar, and one hundred-dollar bills. Challenge students to make given amounts using the fewest bills possible.

**Probability**—Give each student colored counters, chips, or squares. Provide 5 red, 3 blue, and 2 green. Have students place their counters in a bag. Ask them to predict which color they think they will pick most often. Then without looking, have them each pick a counter from the bag and record its color. Have them put the counters back in the bag, shake it, and repeat the process 10 times. Have them compare the results with their predictions. Experiment with other proportions of counters, for example 2, 2, and 2.

## Sample Math Activities

The following are tried and true activities that work well in fifth grade.

### Long Division

When doing long division, the students should show their work to clearly demonstrate whether they understand each step involved. Letting students work out the problems on graph paper helps them to space out their problems neatly. The family approach listed below gives the students helpful reminders of the steps of long division.

| | | |
|---|---|---|
| Step 1. Divide | = | **Dad** |
| Step 2. Multiply | = | **Mom** |
| Step 3. Subtract | = | **Sister** |
| Step 4. Check | = | **Cat** |
| Step 5. Bring down | = | **Brother** |

> ## TIP!
> *Ask open-ended questions that require students to organize data, evaluate possible solutions, and make decisions.*

Remind students to repeat all steps beginning with step one and continue until they run out of "brothers" or "brother" is smaller than the divisor. He then becomes a remainder.

Some students may be in the habit of placing a zero above the first number(s) of the dividend to indicate that the divisor does not go into the dividend. Although correct, it is preferable to have them mark an X instead. Tell them that this helps them to remember step two.

### Symmetry

Understanding symmetry is an important geometry skill. Here are a few ways to help your students with symmetry.

**Missing Half**—Have students look through magazines and find pictures that are symmetrical. Large, full-page pictures work well for this project. Students fold the pictures along the lines of symmetry and then cut along the lines. Have students glue one half of the picture onto a piece of construction paper and use crayons or colored pencils to draw the missing half of the picture.

**Snowflakes**—With this activity, students discover that snowflakes are symmetrical and have more than one line of symmetry. Provide scissors and plain white paper cut into squares. Demonstrate how to fold a square into a triangle and then fold that triangle in half. Then have students fold their papers, and cut different shapes out of the sides of the triangles. When unfolded, these will become snowflakes with two lines of symmetry. Once students become proficient, you might want to experiment with origami paper or squares of wrapping paper to add color to this project.

> **Learning is not just knowing the answer, it's knowing how to find the answer.**

### Money Management

Collect grocery store advertisements to use for this real-life math activity. You may want to have students work in pairs or small groups. Provide each group with a grocery store advertisement and give each group a different task. Examples are listed below.

- You have $20.00 to spend. Plan a balanced dinner for a family of five.

- You have $75.00 to spend for a week's worth of groceries. What will you buy?

### Algebra

Fifth graders can tackle simple algebra. Set up easy problems for them to think about such as $X + 3 = 5$. If you tell them to think of the equal sign as a fulcrum and the equation as the board of a teeter-totter, they will soon get the idea that the board needs to remain balanced. One side is equal to the other side. Using this approach, they recognize that $X$ represents the number $2$.

> **TIP!**
>
> *Manipulatives allow students of all ability levels to extend their thinking through concrete experiences.*

### Geometry

Use concrete items found in the classroom as models for geometric concepts. Introduce the symbols for point, line segment, line, ray, parallel lines, angle, perpendicular lines, and plane. Models found in the classroom are the corner tips of a page, the fold in a piece of paper, etc. Typical geometric topics covered in fifth grade are scalene, isosceles, and equilateral triangles; acute and obtuse angles; prisms; pyramids; faces; vertices; edges; and similar figures.

### Prime Numbers

A prime number has exactly two factors. The factors are itself and 1. Provide a blank chart with the numbers 1 to 100 (found on page 41) and colored markers. Then give these directions:

1. Shade in all the boxes with numbers that are divisible by the number 2 using a red marker.

2. Use a blue marker to circle the number 3 and every third number after it.

3. With the green marker, cross out the number 5 and all multiples of five (any number ending in zero or five).

4. Outline the number 7 in purple and every seventh number after 7 on the chart.

5. Cross out the number 1 because it is not considered a prime number.

6. The first four prime numbers are 2, 3, 5, and 7. Every number left on the chart that has not been colored is a prime number. You should have 25 prime numbers.

As a follow up activity, have students write about the patterns they see. Ask *Which multiples form columns? Which multiples form diagonals? Is there a rule for each pattern?*

# Numbers 1 to 100

| 1 | 2 | 3 | 4 | 5 | 6 | 7 | 8 | 9 | 10 |
|---|---|---|---|---|---|---|---|---|---|
| 11 | 12 | 13 | 14 | 15 | 16 | 17 | 18 | 19 | 20 |
| 21 | 22 | 23 | 24 | 25 | 26 | 27 | 28 | 29 | 30 |
| 31 | 32 | 33 | 34 | 35 | 36 | 37 | 38 | 39 | 40 |
| 41 | 42 | 43 | 44 | 45 | 46 | 47 | 48 | 49 | 50 |
| 51 | 52 | 53 | 54 | 55 | 56 | 57 | 58 | 59 | 60 |
| 61 | 62 | 63 | 64 | 65 | 66 | 67 | 68 | 69 | 70 |
| 71 | 72 | 73 | 74 | 75 | 76 | 77 | 78 | 79 | 80 |
| 81 | 82 | 83 | 84 | 85 | 86 | 87 | 88 | 89 | 90 |
| 91 | 92 | 93 | 94 | 95 | 96 | 97 | 98 | 99 | 100 |

# PHYSICAL EDUCATION

Physical education instruction in fifth grade focuses on giving students many opportunities to improve self-image as more complex manipulative and rhythmic skills are perfected. In fifth grade, students have a wide range of abilities. As you develop your physical education program, provide activities designed to produce the physical education skills listed below.

- Leap while catching a basketball rebounding off the backboard.
- Use a proper sprinter's start.
- Run the 50-yard dash demonstrating good form.
- Use good style while finishing dashes.
- Jump Double Dutch with jump ropes.
- Shoot a ball for a basket in basketball.
- Catch a basketball pass above the waist.
- Catch a basketball pass below the waist.
- Pass a football five yards.
- Center a football with accuracy.
- Catch a football while running.
- Catch a kickball above the waist.
- Catch a kickball below the waist.
- Dribble a ball with the feet.
- Dribble and trap a ball with the feet while moving around cones.
- Serve a volleyball over the net.
- Return a volleyball over the net without throwing.
- Pass a baton in a relay.
- Pass a soccer ball with the foot.

- Practice catching a softball thrown above the waist.
- Place-kick a football.
- Attempt to shoot a foul shot from the free throw line.
- Listen and act out complex cues that are given.
- Perform a grapevine step.
- Practice doing a two-step.
- Practice doing a polka step.
- Perform tricks on circular traveling rings.
- Explain health principles related to exercise, cleanliness, and avoiding illness.
- Understand the importance of self-image.
- Understand and explain that people have differing physical structures and abilities.
- Realize that focused practice can lead to success.
- Give one's best effort toward meeting group goals.
- Invent games with a group.
- Demonstrate a dance, game, or stunt.
- Assist in the organization of some physical education lessons.
- Teach games that are played in the classroom.
- Teach a skill to a small group.
- Plan personal recreational activities.

## TIP!

*NEVER give up recess! It is absolutely essential for the physical, social, and intellectual growth of every child.*

## Physical Fitness Test

During fifth grade, many states require a physical fitness test which may include a sit and reach test, a pull-up test, a sit-up test, and a one-mile run/walk test. Check with your school or district for specific details for your state.

## Warm-Ups

tress the importance of proper warm-ups before hysical activity to help prevent injury. All of these tanding exercises can be done outdoors or ndoors. If your facility permits, adding push-ups, it-ups, or chin-ups to this routine is beneficial.

Butterfly Stroke—Standing with feet a few inches apart, stretch out arms to the sides and rotate arms in large circles. Start with 10 of these and increase to 20.

• Neck Rotation—Slowly rotate your head to the right and then to the left. Repeat. Then nod your head slowly forward and backward. Slowly move your head in a full circle in one direction and then reverse the direction. Do 5 of these. (This is a good relaxation technique to do in class before exams.)

• Hamstring Stretch—Cross one leg in front of the other. Slowly bend forward at the waist and try to touch the toes. Keep the rear leg straight and the heel on the ground. Relax and hold for 15 seconds. Repeat stretch with the other leg in front. Do two to three of these.

• Half Squat—Starting with hands on hips, extend arms forward while bending knees to a half-squat (thighs are parallel to the floor). Hold this position for several seconds and then slowly come back up. Repeat 8–10 times.

## Cool-Downs

Stress the importance of cooling down after physical activity. Walking for several minutes and repeating one of the warm-up exercises is a good way to cool down.

## Balls

Give your students many opportunities to practice their skills with basketballs, footballs, kickballs, soccer balls, volleyballs, and softballs.

## Dashes

Help your students practice the 50-yard dash demonstrating good form. Good form is landing on the heel of the foot, rolling the foot forward, and pushing off with each stride, running tall with a straight back, head held up, and knees slightly bent. The arms should pump in a relaxed motion and be held close to the body with the elbows bent. The shoulders are level and the hands are relaxed.

> **Nothing is a waste of time if you use the experience wisely.**
>
> —**Auguste Rodin**

## Square Dancing

Square dancing is an enjoyable physical education activity. There are several super square dancing compact discs that you can use to teach square dancing. *Square Dancing Made Easy* by Slim Jackson (Audio CD, 1996), *Square Dances—Music and Calls* (Audio CD, 1992), and *Square Dance Tonight* (Audio CD, 1993).

### *The Noble Duke of York*

Set up: Four couples (eight dancers) form two lines facing each other about five to six feet apart. Traditionally boys stand in one line and girls in the other. This is called the set. The head couple is at the top of the set nearest the music and the foot couple is at the opposite end of the set.

*Directions:*

1. The head boy and the head girl move into the area between the two facing lines and join inside hands. They walk eight steps through the set toward the foot couple.

2. The two students in the middle turn to face each other, join the other hands, and walk back to the head of the set.

3. The same couple joins both hands and skips down the center of the set.

4. At the foot of the set, the couple forms an arch with their arms.

5. The new head girl leads her line along the outside of her side of the set and the new head boy leads his line along the outside of his side of the set and they meet at the far side of the arch.

6. As partners meet, they join hands, go under the arch, and walk or skip back to their places.

Repeat this dance until all the couples have had the opportunity to be the head couple. Once the steps are mastered, have students dance to a recorded version of *The Noble Duke of York*. One recorded version is by Ed McCurdy on *Children's Songs: The Greatest Hits* (Audio CD, 1993).

## Buffalo Gals

Set up: Couples hold each other in a traditional dance position and form a circle with the girls on the outside and boys on the inside of the circle.

*Directions:*

1. Begin with the heel-and-toe step. Girls extend their right feet and place their heels on the ground with their toes pointing up. Boys do the same step with their left feet.

2. Each dancer brings the extended leg back and touches the floor with the toe.

3. All repeat the heel-and-toe step one more time.

4. Everyone takes four sliding steps to the girls' right. The circle should move in unison.

5. Next, all repeat the heel-and-toe step two times with the opposite leg.

6. Everyone takes four sliding steps to the girls' left.

7. Partners face each other, drop arms, and clap their right hands three times, then their left hands together three times, and finally both of their hands three times.

8. Each partner slaps his or her knees three times.

9. Partners link right elbows and walk around each other once in a clockwise direction.

10. Partners say goodbye as each boy moves one girl to the left.

11. The dance is repeated with the new partner.

The verbal call directions are:

*Heel and Toe, Heel and Toe*
*Slide, slide, slide, and slide*
*Heel and Toe, Heel and Toe*
*Slide, slide, slide, and slide*
*Right clap, clap, clap*
*Left clap, clap, clap*
*Both clap, clap, clap*
*Knees slap, slap, slap*
*Right elbows circle and move on to the next.*

nce the steps are mastered, you may want to play recorded version of *Buffalo Gals*. See reference to quare dancing music at the beginning of this ction.

# SCIENCE AND HEALTH

## Science

ience instruction in fifth grade focuses on the udents' participation in problem-solving and vestigating scientific concepts. Scientists study he natural world and propose explanations based n evidence from their work by doing inquiries. tudents should be encouraged to engage in cientific inquiries. Inquiries work best when udents seek answers by making observations, osing questions, examining books and other ources of information to find out what is already nown, planning experiments, using tools to nterpret data, proposing explanations and redictions, and communicating their results. As ou develop your science program, try to place an mphasis on doing science in a way that promotes nquiry, experimentation, and learning rather than n just coming up with the right answer. Although pecific science topics vary from state to state, ome general skills to address in fifth grade are isted below.

- Collect and process data by exploring and examining objects or sequencing events.

- Seek, describe, and evaluate the explanatory ideas of others concerning natural phenomena.

- Predict and draw inferences.

- Design or plan appropriate investigations with controls and a variable to support or refute a hypothesis.

- Recognize the difference between hypotheses and factual data based on investigations.

- Generate, record, interpret, and analyze data.

- Verify and evaluate data obtained by repeating investigations.

- Summarize experiences and apply the knowledge to other situations.

- Demonstrate care when handling materials and chemicals.

- Use metric and U.S. customary weights and measures.

- Select and use science textbooks, reading references, and media materials to gather data and develop ideas.

- Utilize appropriate reading skills in comprehending science content.

- Develop a science vocabulary.

## Science Safety

The major causes of science accidents are inattention, carelessness, and unsafe behavior. Conduct a visual safety tour of the classroom. Point out the location of safety equipment and demonstrate the proper use of protective eye equipment and how to properly note the odor of a chemical. Then review the safety guidelines in the chart with your students.

> **The world looks so different after learning science.**
>
> **For example, trees are made of air, primarily. When they are burned, they go back to air, and in the flaming heat is released the flaming heat of the sun which was bound in to convert the air into tree. [A]nd in the ash is the small remnant of the part which did not come from air, that came from the solid earth, instead.**
>
> **These are beautiful things, and the content of science is wonderfully full of them. They are very inspiring, and they can be used to inspire others.**
>
> **—Richard Feynman**

**45**

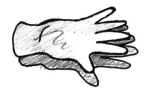

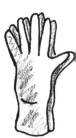

# SAFETY GUIDELINES

- Tie back long hair or loose clothing when working with flames.

- If a fire starts, do not run or panic. Cover the area with a fire blanket and notify the teacher.

- Look for all safety warnings before doing an activity.

- Do not touch hot glassware.

- Use caution with all hot liquids.

- Wear eye protection when working with open flames or chemicals, or when doing any activity that could harm the eyes.

- Do not shine direct sunlight into the eyes with a magnifier or mirror.

- Examine all glassware before using.

- Do not use broken or chipped glassware.

- Keep your work area clear except for science materials.

- Clean up before leaving the class.

- Put away all materials where instructed.

- Do not throw chemicals into the sink unless instructed by the teacher.

- Never taste a chemical unless instructed to do so.

- Never directly smell any chemical. Instead wave the chemical in the air, directing the smell toward your nose.

- If any chemical is spilled, notify the teacher immediately.

- Do not run or play in the laboratory.

- Notify the teacher of an accident or any broken equipment immediately

**46**
reproducible FS122007 Getting Ready to Teach Fifth Grade

## The Scientific Method

Explain the scientific method to your students. The scientific method is a way of thinking. Not all scientists use all of the steps, and the steps may be sometimes used out of order.

Step 1— Choose a problem and state it in the form of a question.

Step 2— Research what is already know.

Step 3— Develop a hypothesis based on the information you gathered.

Step 4— Test your hypothesis by doing an experiment and collecting observations in the form of data.

Step 5— Analyze or study your data.

Step 6— Based on your data, make a conclusion whether your hypothesis is correct or not. If it is not correct, it must be changed and retested.

Step 7— Communicate your results. Other scientists may repeat the experiment to see if they get the same results or they may find ways to apply the findings to their own work.

## Physical Science

Physical science experiences in fifth grade should help students develop an understanding of properties and changes of properties in matter, motions and forces, and transfer of energy. Here are some ideas that work well.

### Changes in Matter

Matter can go through physical and chemical changes. In a physical change, the matter's shape, weight, or other physical properties may change, but the molecules of the matter do not change. The matter usually can be returned to its original form. In a chemical change, the molecules of the matter change to other kinds of molecules, forming a new substance.

The following experiment demonstrates how carbon dioxide is created when vinegar and baking soda are combined.

> **Our young people must be exposed to science both because it is useful and because it is fun. Both of these qualities should be taken at a truly high value.**
>
> —Edward Teller, <u>Conversations on the Dark Secrets of Physics</u>, 1991

**Materials:** two 12-ounce plastic soda bottles, two balloons, baking soda, tablespoon, funnel ¼ cup vinegar, ¼ cup water

**Predictions:** Students predict what will happen when baking soda is mixed with water and then with vinegar.

**Procedure:** Students pour the water into a bottle and use a funnel to put a tablespoon of baking soda in a balloon. Then they stretch the balloon around the neck of the bottle and lift the balloon so the baking soda drops into the water. Then they repeat the activity using vinegar instead of water.

**Results:** Students draw a diagram and write about what happened each time they added the baking soda.

**Discovery:** The students will discover that a chemical change occurs when vinegar and baking soda are combined. The vinegar and baking soda combine to form carbon dioxide, a gas. The gas molecules cause the balloon to inflate. When the baking soda and water are combined, the balloon does not inflate because no gas is formed.

### Force and Motion

A force is a push or pull. A force is needed to make an object that is not moving start to move, or to make a moving object speed up, slow down, or stop. Objects in motion or at rest tend to stay that way unless acted upon by an outside force.

The following activity demonstrates the principle that objects at rest tend to stay at rest unless acted upon by an outside force.

**Materials:** a plastic cup, a smooth sheet of paper, a flat table surface

**Predictions:** Students predict what will happen to a cup if a piece of paper is pulled out from under it.

**Procedure:** Students place a sheet of paper on the edge of the table so that half of the paper hangs over the table's edge. Then they place the cup on the paper that is on the table. Then students stand at the edge of the table and quickly pull the paper toward themselves.

**Results:** Students draw pictures showing what happened during the experiment and write about it.

**Discovery:** The students will discover that the cup will remain in place on the table.

**TIP!**

*It's better to study in depth a few things that students will remember and appreciate than to overwhelm them with facts they will soon forget.*

### Magnetism

Magnets pick up or attract things containing iron or steel. Magnetic force can pass through many materials. A magnet has two poles—north and south. When two magnets are close to each other, opposite poles attract and like poles repel. A magnet can be used to make an object containing iron or steel act as a magnet.

Students build their own magnets and test them with the following activity.

**Materials:** bar magnets, darning needles, large corks, shallow plastic bowls, liquid detergent, plastic spoons, water

**Predictions:** Students predict what will happen when a needle stroked against a magnet and pushed through a cork is placed in a bowl of water.

**Procedure:** Each student carefully holds a needle and strokes it in one direction on the bar magnet for 40 or more times. Then the needle is pushed through the middle of the cork. The bowl is filled with water and three drops of the liquid detergent are added to the water and stirred. Students float the cork-needle in the center of the bowl of water to see what happens.

**Results:** Students draw pictures showing what happened and write about it.

**Discovery:** Students will discover that the corks and needles turn in the water. (If they do not, students need to stroke the needles along the magnets again.) If real compasses are available, you may want the students to check their cork compasses and record the direction they are pointing. NOTE: If the two compasses come too close together, they will affect each other.

### Transfer of Energy

Energy is a property of many substances and is associated with heat, light, electricity, mechanical motion, sound, nuclei, and the nature of a chemical. Energy is transferred in many ways.

The following activity demonstrates that sound waves travel farther through solids and liquids than through gases.

**Materials:** softly ticking clock, watch or timer, wooden table, ruler

**Predictions:** Students will predict whether sound travels better through air or wood.

**Procedure:** Students each place the objects near their ears to hear the ticking, then slowly move the tickers away until the ticking can no longer be heard. Students measure the distance from the objects to their ears. Next, they place the objects face down on the table(s), and rest their ears next to them. Students slowly move the ticking objects away until the ticking can no longer be heard. Again they measure the distances from the objects to their ears.

**Results:** Students record the measurements they make.

**Discovery:** Students should be able to hear the clock from a greater distance through the wood than through the air. Sound waves travel farther through solids and liquids than through gases because the molecules in solids and liquids are more densely packed than the molecules in gases.

## Life Science

Life science experiences in fifth grade should help students develop an understanding of the structure and function in living systems, reproduction and heredity, regulation and behavior, populations and ecosystems, and diversity and adaptations of organisms. Here are some ideas that work well.

> **We cannot create observers by saying "observe," but by giving them the power and the means for this observation, and these means are procured through education of the senses.**
>
> **—Maria Montessori**

### Cells

All organisms are composed of cells—the fundamental unit of life. Most organisms are single cells. Other organisms, including human, are multicellular. Cells carry on the many functions needed to sustain life. They grow and divide, thereby producing more cells. This requires that they take in nutrients, which they use to provide energy for the work they do and to make the materials that a cell or an organism needs.

The following activity demonstrates how the cell membrane allows some substances to enter but does not allow starch particles to pass through.

**Materials:** cornstarch, tablespoon, clear plastic bag, twist tie, two glasses, iodine, test tube, eyedropper

**Predictions:** Students will predict if a starch and water solution and an iodine and water solution will pass through a plastic bag.

**Procedure:** Students will mix a tablespoon of cornstarch with eight ounces of water and place that mixture in a plastic bag and secure it with a twist tie. They will wash off the bag to make sure none of the solution is on the outside of the bag. Next, the students will mix eight ounces of water with 10 drops of iodine in a clean glass. Then the bag with the cornstarch solution is placed in the glass with the iodine and water mixture. The students will observe any changes that occur in the next hour.

**Results:** Students record their observations.

**Discovery:** Students discover that the solution in the plastic bag turns black because the iodine solution entered the bag and mixed with the starch. (Iodine turns black in the presence of starch.) The iodine solution outside the bag does not turn black because the starch molecules are too big to pass through the pores in the bag.

Tell the class that the bag represents the cell membrane that allows certain molecules to pass through. Explain that the movement of one liquid from one solution into another through a membrane is called *osmosis*.

## Animal Adaptations

Living things can respond to the challenges of their environment with changes and variations in form and behavior.

The following activity lets students discover that birds have specialized beaks that enable them to eat the types of food that they need.

**Materials:** crochet hook, tweezers, nutcracker, walnuts, cotton balls, sponges

**Procedure:** The students will use each of the three tools (crochet hook, tweezer, nutcracker) to try to crack open a walnut, catch a cotton ball in midair, and tear off a small chunk of sponge.

**Results:** Students will write a description of what happened each time they tried each task.

**Discovery:** The students will discover the following:

1. The nutcracker works best for opening the walnut. It is similar to the beak of a bird that eats seeds or nuts.

2. The crochet hook works best for tearing off a chunk of sponge. It represents the hooked beak needed by a predator for tearing meat.

3. The tweezers work to catch a cotton ball in the same way that the pointed beak of an insect-eating bird works to catch insects.

## Studying Traits

Ask the students to name some physical features that help distinguish them from their friends (examples: hair, skin, and eye colors; height; weight; facial features). Discuss why people do not look alike. Tell students that people generally look the way they do because of certain characteristics or traits they inherited from their parents. Explain that this passing on of characteristics is called heredity.

In this activity, students will look at different traits and compare themselves based on the traits studied.

**Procedure:** Students work with partners to see which traits they have in common. First, have each student answer the questions below:

1. Can your roll up the edges of your tongue?
2. Do you have a widow's peak?
3. Is the last segment of your thumb straight?
4. Do you have free earlobes?
5. Is your hair naturally curly?
6. Do you have dimples?
7. Do you have a cleft in your chin?
8. Fold your hands. Which thumb is on top?
9. What color are your eyes?

**Results:** The students share their findings with the class and make a class graph to see which traits are the most commonly shared in the classroom.

**Discovery:** Students discover that some physical attributes in humans are more common than others.

## Food Webs

All organisms have roles in the ecosystem. They may eat other animals, serve as food for other species, or shelter or decompose other organisms. Some may have more than one role.

### TIP!

*Research shows that most teachers wait only one second for answers to their questions. When they waited 3 - 5 seconds, more students participated in discussions.*

Have students work in pairs to research one of the following organisms using animal books or encyclopedias: crab, phytoplankton, sperm whale, anchovy, flying fish, killer whale, dolphin, shark, zooplankton, squid, tuna, seabird, salmon, blue whale, hatchetfish. Have them find out what role their organism plays in the food web and what would be the effect of removing it from the web. Have the pairs of students present their findings to the class.

## Earth Science

Earth science experiences in fifth grade should help students develop an understanding of the structure of the earth, the history of the earth, and the earth as part of the solar system. Here are some sample lessons.

### Changes in the Earth's Surface

Weathering is the breaking up of rocks by natural forces such as water, ice, temperature changes, plants, and chemicals. Erosion is a slow wearing, washing, or eating away. Weathering and erosion act on rocks and minerals to change landforms, and create soil.

The following activity demonstrates how heavy rains affect soil and its nutrients.

**Materials:** soil, red food coloring, paper cup, plastic spoon, funnel, glass jar, basket-style coffee filter, water

**Predictions:** Students predict what will happen when water is poured into a filter that contains soil mixed with food coloring.

**Procedure:** Students fill the paper cups with soil, add five drops of red food coloring to the soil, and mix well. Next, students place the funnels into the mouths of the glass jars, arrange the coffee filters in the funnels, and add the colored soil to the filters. Then students pour 1/2 cup water into the filter and observe the results. Then add another 1/2 cup of water and observe again.

**Results:** Students record their observations.

**Discovery:** The soil contains nutrients that are soluble in water. When it rains heavily, the nutrients (represented by the red food coloring) are washed away and over time the soil becomes infertile.

### Fossils

Fossils are the remains of plants and animals preserved in rock. These plants and animals lived millions of years ago. Some fossils are leaves, bones, teeth, or shells preserved after the plant or animal died. Other fossils are tracks that were left by animals moving across mud.

In this activity, students make their own models of fossils. This activity requires plaster. To ease in cleaning, you may want to make the plaster (according to package directions) in a two-liter plastic soda bottle that has the top cut off. Since plaster hardens very quickly, you'll want to make sure all students are ready for the plaster before you mix it. Never pour plaster into sinks or drains since it may clog plumbing.

> **It is better to ask some of the questions than to know all of the answers.**
>
> —James Thurber, The James Thurber Carnival

**Materials:** assorted shells, petroleum jelly, baby powder, non-hardening clay, plaster, water, two-liter plastic soda bottle with top cut off, spoon, toothpick

**Procedure:** Each student places a small amount of petroleum jelly spread evenly on the outside of a shell. Next, each student makes a ball of clay slightly bigger than the shell and presses the shell into the clay to make an impression then puts a thin layer of baby powder into the impression. Pour plaster into each student's shell impression. Once the plaster is slightly hardened, students can write their names in it with a toothpick. Leave the clay and plaster to dry overnight. The next day, students carefully remove the plaster from the clay and compare the shells, the clay impressions, and the plaster pieces.

**Discovery:** Students discover that the cast looks very much like the original shell. Tell your class that fossils form in different ways. One type of fossil is formed when a plant or animal part has been buried in clay or mud that has turned to stone. Over time, water dissolves the plant or animal part, leaving a hollow space in the shape of the organism. This hollow space is called a mold. Sometimes a cast is formed when water containing dissolved mineral fills the mold. When the mineral deposits harden, they form a cast, an exact copy of the original plant or animal part.

> **TIP!**
>
> *Instructional television (ITV) can enrich the curriculum and motivate students to learn. Consult your local school district to find out how to access ITV in your community.*

Tell your students that scientists use fossils as clues about what kinds of organisms existed long ago and what their surroundings were like.

### The Seasons

The seasons result from variations in the amount of the sun's energy hitting the surface of the earth, due to the tilt of the earth's rotation on its axis.

The following activity demonstrates how the earth's tilt affects the strength of the sunlight a part of the earth receives.

**Materials:** masking tape, cup, flashlight, inflated balloon with line drawn around the middle and an **X** mark midway between the line and the top of the balloon

**Predictions:** Students will predict if a spot on a balloon will get stronger light when it is tilted toward a flashlight or when it is tilted away from the flashlight.

**Procedure:** Students stand the balloons in the cups on tables. Then they place strips of tape on tables a few inches in front of the cups. (The **X**s on the balloons should be facing the tape strips.) Next, they tilt the top of the balloons toward the tape strips, holding the flashlights even with the tape strips to shine lights on the **X** marks. Then they will tilt the balloons away from the tape strips and shine the flashlights on the **X** marks again.

**Results:** Students draw pictures and write about their observations.

**Discovery:** Students discover that when the balloons are tilted toward the flashlights, the light is concentrated over smaller areas than when the balloons are tilted away from the flashlights. This model shows the concentration of light that the earth gets depends on the tilt of the earth's rotation on its axis.

# Health

Health instruction in fifth grade should provide students with many opportunities for problem-solving situations which allow them to make decisions and develop important skills. Although health can be integrated with other areas of the curriculum, some specific skills to address in fifth grade are listed below.

Maintain appropriate health, grooming, and cleanliness.

Identify benefits of physical exercise.

Define wellness.

Describe the relationship between personal lifestyle choices and one's level of wellness.

Identify risk factors to reduce cardiovascular disorders.

Recognize the value of medical examinations and dental checkups.

Protect the skin from sunburn.

Discuss the role of the family in an individual's development.

Recognize changing attitudes toward gender roles and career opportunities.

Differentiate between inherited and acquired traits.

Understand the physical and emotional changes which occur during puberty and identify the fertility cycle and menstruation. (Requires parental consent.)

Maintain acceptable social standards when eating alone or in groups.

Interpret information contained on food package labels.

Demonstrate ability to make food choices according to nutrient content.

Classify foods according to groups, textures, sources, and ethnic background.

Explain how a variety of foods contributes to health and growth.

- Explain why nutrition requirements vary from person to person.

- Maintain respect for similarities and differences between and among individuals and groups.

- Relate choices to short-term and long-term consequences.

- Describe ways to handle upset feelings.

- Apply steps in decision-making to resolve problems.

- Accept responsibility for own actions.

- Describe positive personality traits.

- Explain the influence of peer pressure on behavior.

- Identify consequences of substance abuse.

- Identify ways in which the media influences decision making.

- Indicate how personal values influence decisions to use or not use specific substances.

- Analyze activities that provide satisfaction.

- Recognize and resist pressures to experiment with substances.

- Distinguish those diseases caused by microorganisms from diseases resulting from other factors.

- Recognize the major diseases affecting people.

- Identify scientific contributions that have been made to help protect people from diseases and disorders.

- Identify procedures for locating community resources that protect and promote individual, family, and community health.

> **With good heredity nature deals you a fine hand at cards; and with a good environment, you can learn to play the hand well.**
>
> **—Walter C. Alvarez, M.D.**

- Explain how local, state, and national laws and regulations affect the health of the community.

- Describe methods used to control environmental pollution.

- Identify different careers from the health-care field.

- Identify common techniques and underlying messages in advertisements.

- Differentiate between good and bad touching.

- List steps taken if someone touches a person in a way that makes them feel uncomfortable.

- Maintain precautions for self-protection in public places.

- Identify reasons for immediate care in cases of emergencies.

- Recognize and practice appropriate behavior during emergency drills.

- Explain the importance of taking responsibility for the safety of self and others.

## Sample Ideas

### Drug Education

Many police departments offer a drug education program. As part of some programs, police officers come to your class on an on-going basis to educate your students on the dangers of drug use. Check with your local police department to see if such a program is offered.

### Question Box

In fifth grade, students are becoming aware of the changes they observe in their bodies and in their peers. Students may feel uncomfortable asking health questions in front of the class. Provide a question box that students can use to anonymously ask questions. Ignore any inappropriate questions that may appear. Read the appropriate questions aloud and lead the class in discussions.

### Special Topics

During fifth grade, most schools require a introduction to puberty and menstruation. Paren permission is usually required for students t participate. You may want to hold a special sessio for parents to attend so they are familiar with wha their children will be learning. Separate session for boys and girls allows them to ask question more freely and to better concentrate on th subject matter. Students at this age have a natura tendency to laugh when they hear something tha is uncomfortable to them. Acknowledging thi beforehand is helpful.

Subject matter is best approached in an open an mature manner. Restrict the talk to puberty, thei changing bodies, and menstruation. Specifi questions regarding sex should be referred to hom and their parents. Using correct terminology is als important. Since all students will experienc puberty at different times, use examples from thei childhood to help reinforce the idea of staggerec development. For example, some of us learned tc walk before we were one year old, some of u. learned a little later, but eventually we all learned.

# SOCIAL STUDIES

The social studies curriculum in fifth grade offer endless possibilities for classroom activities anc research projects. As you plan your social studie: program, think about providing interdisciplinar. experiences that allow students to develop specifi social studies skills that can be applied to everyday living. Some specific skills to address in fifth grade are listed below.

- Interpret facts and form opinions.

- Interpret and evaluate ideas.

- Locate and acquire information from multimedia sources.

- Develop simple business letters for obtaining information.

- Locate pertinent information from various reading sources, using library catalogues and atlases.

Use parts of the book to find information, including the index.

Select and compare information acquired from various sources.

Discriminate between primary and secondary source materials and make selection based on type of information needed.

Answer questions related to specific topics and units of study using complete sentences.

Create and participate in various activities involving a study of people, events, and ideas.

Place directives, processes, or procedures in sequential order.

Take part in discussions, expressing one's ideas and concerns, or extending the ideas to others.

Write lists, make graphs, use illustrations to summarize information.

Paraphrase information and present orally in written paragraphs or dramatizations.

Write facts under prepared outline headings.

Classify words according to category.

Cite omissions and distortions in accounts of the roles and achievements of racial and cultural groups in American history.

Use indefinite time concepts in discussions, in written, and in oral work.

Recognize and apply map and globe concepts and terms such as the following: boundary or territory, distance, hemisphere, equator, time zone, and sphere.

Identify, describe, and use major parts of a map such as the title, scale, and grid.

Identify, describe, and read various maps such as resource, product, transportation, population, political, vegetation, and relief.

**TIP!**

*Introduce your students to newspapers as a source of up-to-date information.*

- Interpret and categorize given information from charts, tables, graphs, and diagrams.

- Prepare and interpret time lines from given information or individually researched information.

- Place facts and events in chronological order.

- Analyze information or messages contained in various posters and political cartoons.

- Compare and explain ideas contained in various sources.

- Predict the outcome of a particular behavior and discuss possible consequences.

- Use sequence and chronology in discussion.

- Demonstrate conceptual understanding about the unity of study, showing relationship among several concepts.

- Apply information to new situations.

- Infer and give reasons for inferences.

- Analyze cause and effect relationships among political, social, and economic events.

- Identify steps in the problem-solving method.

- Recognize that there is a problem.

- Represent the problem.

- Identify or devise various solutions.

- Select and execute the solution plan.

- Evaluate the solution.

- Demonstrate the following values when working individually or participating in group activities: integrity, justice, reverence, love, respect for law and order.

**Education is not the filling of a pail, but the lighting of a fire.**

**—William Butler Yeats**

## Sample Outline

This outline can be used to help students plan their reports.

I. Introduction
  A. Name of state
  B. Nicknames and state symbols
  C. Statehood
  D. Current population

II. Geography
  A. Location and size
  B. Physical features
  C. Climate
  D. Hand drawn map
    1. Capital, major cities
    2. Rivers, lakes
    3. Landforms

III. History
  A. Native Americans
  B. Exploration and settlement
  C. Events of the 1800's
    1.
    2.
    3.
  D. Events of the 1900's
    1.
    2.
    3.

IV. People
  A. Work
    1. Industry
      a.
      b.
    2. Agriculture
      a.
      b.
  B. Famous people
    1. Governor, U.S. Senators
    2. Include at least two others

V. Places of interest (Include at least three.)
  A.
  B.
  C.

VI. Conclusion
  A. Unique features
  B. Personal comments

- Clarify through discussion and/or actions an awareness of one's values, based on such foundations as religious beliefs and family traditions.

- State one or more experiences that may lead to positive changes in values.

- Identify one or more examples of a value conflict related to home and community.

- Identify or state opposing values in a value conflict.

- Demonstrate an ability to interact cooperatively with other persons.

- Recognize that all individuals live within a framework of rules and laws.

- Identify one or more ways in which one's rights may be altered as a result of another's failure to exercise responsibility toward rules and laws.

- Learn the procedures and purposes for voting, and learn about the structure of government.

- Recognize the consumer knowledge needed to make good decisions in the use of individual resources.

- Demonstrate ability to function effectively with various cultural groups.

## Sample Research Projects

**President Report**—Each student selects a president to research. Set a due date and give students guidelines for completing the report.

Sample report guidelines:

- The report should be between 2–3 pages.

- Include a title page with the title of the report, your name, the teacher's name, and the date.

- Include visuals such as maps, time lines, and illustrations.

- If information is taken directly from a book, word for word, you must document with quotation marks and a footnote. Place footnote numbers slightly above the line of text. Number footnote consecutively.

- Include a bibliography at the end of the report. List all the books you used in making your report. Magazines and newspapers are also listed. This list is in alphabetical order by the author's last name.

- Reports may be hand written or typed. Allow ample and even margins. Double-space the text. Indent five spaces for each paragraph. Leave two spaces after periods, question marks, or exclamation points. Place the page number in the upper right-hand corner, two lines after the first line of the text or use a word processor's page numbering system.

Practice writing a title page, footnote, and a bibliography in class so the students will be prepared when they do their final report.

**State Report**—Each student will be engaged in an in-depth study of one of the states of the United States of America. The purposes of this project re to compile factual information about a state and to provide initial basic skill lessons in preparing a research paper through a step-by-step approach. Provide guidelines for completing the report. Sample report guidelines:

- Select a state to study and report on. (This can be any state except for the state studied in fourth grade.)

- The report should be between 6–8 pages.

- Four or more sources are required. Only one may be an encyclopedia. Only one may be an on-line source. You may use nonfiction books, periodicals, or magazines.

- Use note cards to keep a list of sources.

- A complete outline for the entire project is due on _____. (Sample outline in the sidebar on page 56.)

- Write a rough draft of your report. This may be typed or handwritten. Skip lines and write on one side of the paper only. The rough draft is due on _____.

- The final report should be typed or handwritten in ink and will include the following: a creative, original cover, a title page, body (numbered pages, illustrations or pictures, footnotes), and a bibliography. The final report is due on _____.

## Sample Social Studies Activities

### The American Flag

**Famous Flags**—Study the history of famous American flags. Have students research and replicate the following flags to display in the classroom:

| | |
|---|---|
| Colonial Flag | Bunker Hill Flag |
| Navy Jack | Betsy Ross |
| Bennington | John Paul Jones |
| Star-Spangled Banner Flag | 48-Star Flag |
| The third United States Flag | 50-Star Flag |

**Design a Flag**—Have students imagine that we have just added another state to the union. Have them each name the state and design a flag for it.

### The Mayflower

No one knows what the Mayflower looked like, but it was probably about 90 feet long, 64 feet high, and 25 feet wide, with three masts and two decks. It left Plymouth, England, carrying 102 passengers on September 16, 1620. Its destination was Virginia, but bad weather and navigational errors caused the ship to go off course. It dropped anchor off Massachusetts on November 21, 1620.

Have students use their math skills to calculate the following: How many days did the Pilgrims take to arrive in North America? How many miles did the Pilgrims sail? What was the average daily mileage?

Using the dimensions of the Mayflower, have students sketch an outline of the ship using sidewalk chalk on the playground. Imagine and discuss how passengers and crew lived in the space, with no indoor plumbing, with all the supplies the passengers would carry with them to start in a new world where there were no stores, and through stormy weather when many people would be seasick. Have students create journals that could have been written by the passengers or the log kept by the Captain.

### Native Americans

Divide the class into four teams. Have each team represent one of the following Native American Groups:

1. Eastern Woodlands Indians
2. Plains Indians
3. Pacific Northwest Indians
4. Pueblo Indians

> **I have but one lamp by which my feet are guided, and that is the lamp of experience. I know of no way of judging the future, but by the past.**
>
> **—Patrick Henry, Speech (1775)**

A. The teams select a tribe from their group and research the following:

- lifestyle
- beliefs
- family structure
- customs

- technologies
- government
- environment they inhabited
- climate of the area where they lived

B. The teams work together to make models of their homes and draw maps to show where their tribes lived or lives.

C. Compare and contrast the teams' findings on a large class chart. Display a piece of butcher paper. Draw four columns and nine rows. Use the headings and subjects from above to label the chart. Teams can add information to the chart as it is found.

### TIP!

*Arrange desks in small clusters so that eye contact within groups is possible and so that group members can communicate without disturbing others.*

### USA Map Activities

Make copies of the U.S.A. outline map (page 61).

Have students identify and label different copies of the map with the following information.

- each state
- each capital
- regions of the U.S.A.
- boundaries and borders
- major bodies of water
- the Great Lakes
- rivers
- major mountain ranges
- national parks
- original thirteen colonies
- states and capitals

### World Map Activity

Make copies of the world outline map (page 62). Have students identify and label the items on the list below.

- continents
- oceans
- the equator and prime meridian
- hemispheres—north & south and east & west
- countries on a specific continent

### Cardinal Directions

Post the four cardinal directional labels (N, S, E, W) on the corresponding walls of the classroom. Here are some activities to help students practice using these four directional symbols.

- Direct a partner to a certain spot in the classroom.

- Write out directions to other areas of the school. Do they work? Test out your directions with a partner.

- Draw a floor plan of the classroom and include a compass rose.

- Make floor plans of a room in your house and describe its location using cardinal directions.

Add the four intermediate directions (NW, NE, SE, SW) to the classroom walls. Repeat these activities using the four intermediate directions. Then discuss which set of directions was easier to follow? Why?

### Local Maps

Locate your school on a local map. Use this as the starting point for the following activities.

- Give directions to specific locations such as the park, library, mall, or hospital. Can your partner get there following your directions?

- Now try writing directions without disclosing the destination. Can your partner successfully locate the secret spot?

### State Maps

Locate your hometown on a state map. Use this as the starting point for the following activities.

- Locate the state capital, the largest city, the highest point, and the nearest body of water.

- Identify the symbols you see on the map.

- Locate and determine what scale was used to design the map.

### National Maps

Locate a map of the United States. Have students use it for a scavenger hunt to answer the following questions.

1. *Which is the largest state?* (Alaska)

2. *What state is south of Georgia?* (Florida)

3. *Which state is directly south of South Dakota?* (Nebraska)

4. *What state is north of Oregon?* (Washington)

5. *Which is the smallest state?* (Rhode Island)

6. *Which states border California?* (Oregon, Nevada, Arizona)

7. *Which state is farther south Louisiana or Texas?* (Texas)

8. *How many states border Idaho?* (six)

9. *Which state is directly east of Arizona?* (New Mexico)

10. *What is the capital of Illinois?* (Springfield)

As map skills improve the questions can become more complex. Have students create their own scavenger hunts for the class.

### Treasure Hunt

Have students draw a map of a fictional island including a legend, a compass rose, a scale, and a hidden treasure. Tell students to keep the hiding spot a secret. Then have them write out clear directions on another piece of paper and glue them to the back of the map.

Let each mapmaker hold up his or her map and read the directions out loud to a partner. The treasure seeker uses his or her finger to follow the directions to locate the buried treasure.

### Travel Agency

This is a long-term project. Students work in pairs to set up their own travel agencies. Partners select a city that they would like to visit. Then they research and organize information regarding transportation, lodging, places of interest, and restaurants. Students may write to the city's chamber of commerce or travel bureau and request information for the project. Tour books and magazines may be available at the library. Local branches of AAA (The Automobile Club of America) or travel agencies may be able to provide information on the city. The travel section from the newspaper may also be helpful, as would many Internet sites.

> **My idea of education is to unsettle the minds of the young and inflame their intellects.**
>
> **—Robert Hutchins**

## Technology Resources

### Software

*AppleWorks* by Apple Software

Word processing, spreadsheet, database, painting and drawing programs packaged and interactive together for Macintosh computers

*Microsoft Office* by Microsoft

Word processing, spreadsheet, database, painting and drawing programs packaged and interactive together for use by Macintosh or PCs

*HyperStudio* by Roger Wagner Publishing, Inc.

Multimedia authoring tool

*Kid Pix Studio Deluxe* by Brøderbund

Painting, drawing, animation, and fun stuff

*Mavis Beacon Teaches Typing* by The Learning Company

### Resource Books

*Classroom Computer Center Grades 5 and 6* by Concetta Doti Ryan (Frank Schaffer Publications, Inc., 1999)

*Making the Most of the One-Computer Classroom* by Concetta Doti Ryan (Frank Schaffer Publications, Inc., 1999)

Once the research is complete, students do the following.

- Decide on names for the travel agencies.

- Design and make business cards, brochures, travel posters, slogans, and logos.

- Create tour options and package deals for their cities.

Have a travel fair as the culminating event of this project. Invite other classes, family members, and friends to visit and plan their next vacations.

# TECHNOLOGY

## Skills

- Develop standards for interpreting plans and recording data.

- Demonstrate proper use of technology.

- Become familiar with production processes:.

- Develop career awareness relating to job applications and forms, types of work and salaries, and association of skills with types of work.

- Develop positive attitudes about work through hands-on building of projects and working with others to develop projects.

- Gain knowledge in math and problem-solving skills to develop and construct projects successfully.

- Learn the importance of following steps for project construction and interpret data related to project construction.

**TIP!**

*Save time and work by establishing some activities that can go on all year in your classroom.*

Since many businesses and service industries use some kind of electronic communication or data processing device, students must learn to use them in school. The computer and calculator, the electronic cashier's box, and the fax machine are all parts of the world that fifth graders are living in. Having such devices in the classroom, when they help in the actual learning process, is important.

Your students need to develop basic skills with the keyboard and mouse to speed up entering data. There are resource books to help you learn how to use the computer in your classroom. There are great writing and publishing programs. The media specialist or computer lab teacher of your school or district will help you find good software if you are not sure where to begin.

The computer can inspire the most unwilling writer to write, correct, rewrite, and produce interesting illustrations for written presentations. Since a series of rewrites can be stored or printed, the progress of a piece can be seen easily.

# U.S.A. Map

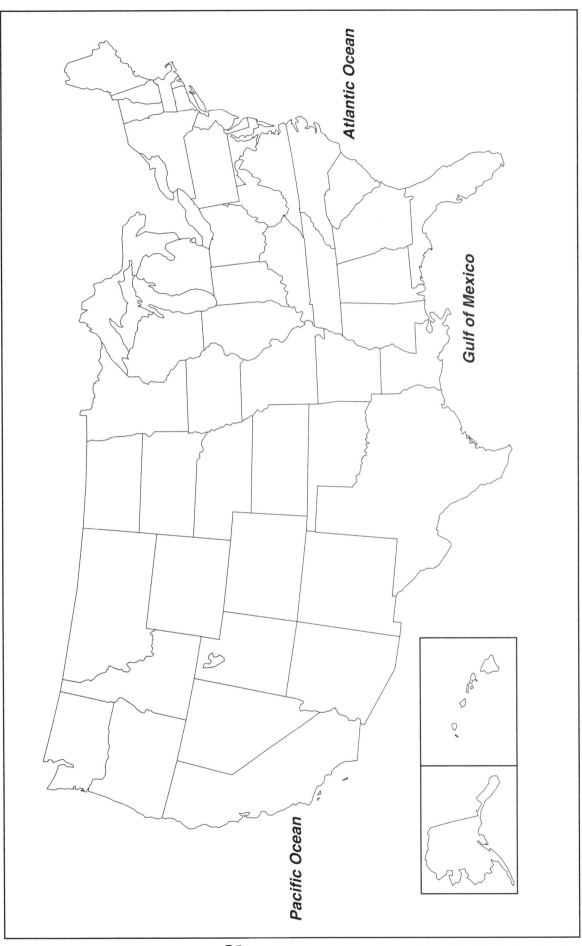

Atlantic Ocean

Gulf of Mexico

Pacific Ocean

Name _____

# World Map

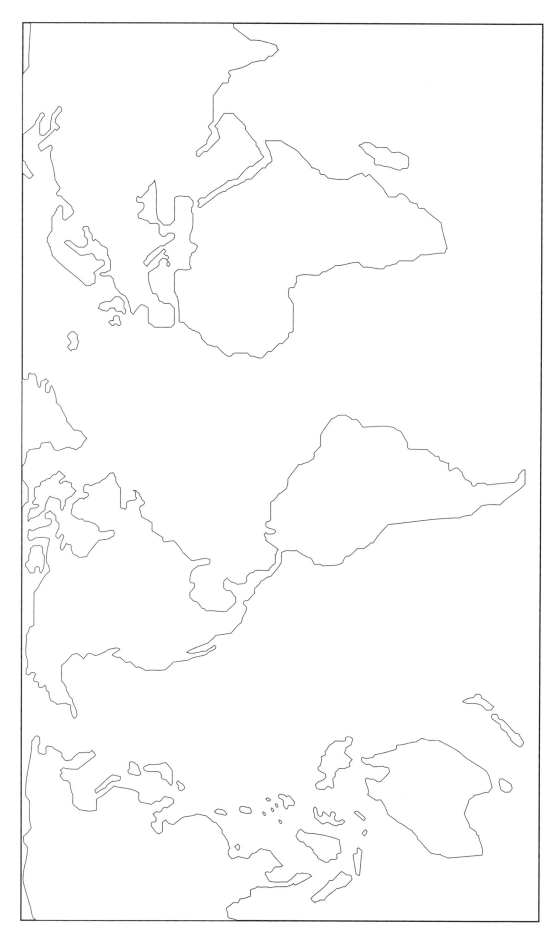

**62**
reproducible

## Sample Projects

### Famous American Bridges

From the Golden Gate Bridge in California to the Brooklyn Bridge in New York, bridges span across the United States. Have students research these and other famous bridges to find examples of as many different types as possible.

Have students work in cooperative groups and hold a bridge-building competition. The winner is the group whose bridge can hold the greatest weight.

**Materials:** toothpicks, craft sticks, glue, paper cups, marbles

**Procedure:** Students decide on the types of bridges to build. Then they draw up plans, gather the necessary materials, and construct the bridges.

Groups present their bridges to the class. Then each crew determines what weight load its bridge can tolerate by placing a paper cup on the bridge, filling it with marbles, and recording how many marbles the bridge can support. Compare results to determine the winning team.

### Let's Go Fly a Kite

Make up individual kite kits ahead of time. Put six plastic flexible straws, six plastic jumbo straws, two pieces of tissue paper, scissors, glue, tape, and a yard of string into each paper lunch bag. Pass out the bags and ask everyone to use the materials to make kites. You'll be surprised by the many different creations your students come up with. If weather permits, let students fly their kites outside.

### Creative Inventions

With this project, students create inventions using only the supplies provided. Make one supply bag for each student. Place a variety of recycled items into each bag. Bags could have the same assortment or they could each hold different surprises.

Suggested materials: buttons, yarn, paper cups, straws, paper tubes, bottle caps, toothpicks, etc.

Allow 45 minutes for students to invent and build contraptions. Have inventors share their inventions with the class to explain how they work.

## Art Vocabulary

Here is a list of terms that will help your students identify and distinguish different kinds of art.

**drawing:** a picture or design created with crayon, chalk, pencil, or ink

**landscape:** a picture of scenery on land

**mosaic:** a picture formed by fitting together small pieces of colored stone, glass, or other materials

**painting:** a picture made by applying pigments and liquid to a surface

**portrait:** a picture of a person

**sculpture:** a design or figure carved or modeled from a hard material, such as stone, metal, or clay

**still life:** a picture of nonliving objects

# VISUAL ARTS AND MUSIC

## Visual Arts

Visual arts experiences in fifth grade should develop students' skills in aesthetic perception, creative expression, aesthetic valuing, and the appreciation of art heritage. The following skills should be included in your visual arts program.

- Analyze color qualities with distinctions of increasing subtlety such as hue, intensity, value, and color relationships.

- Differentiate objects, forms, and expressions as to cultural origins, or historical periods; materials and processes used; art styles, movements, or periods.

- Identify art principles in natural and man-made forms and works of art.

- Demonstrate an increasing acuity of visual recall in oral, written, and visual expressions.

- Identify implied visual movements.

- Depict the three-dimensional qualities indicated by size, color intensity, overlapping planes, and positions in space.

- Perceive and represent objects from various points of view.

**TIP!**

*Make a scrapbook to make an impressive display of samples of students' artwork.*

- Apply descriptive, metaphorical, and visual art terms to discuss visual and tactile characteristics of objects in the environment and works of art.

- Create in both two- and three-dimensional art forms, with appropriate knowledge of the media and processes involved, including drawing, photography, painting, collage, sculpture, crafts, and printmaking.

- Show confidence in pursuing independent activities in the basic expressive media used throughout the preceding grades.

- Demonstrate initiative rather than dependence on teacher direction.

- Organize forms thoughtfully in aesthetically pleasing ways, considering line, color, shape, texture, space, contrast, and balance.

- Visualize and use the total area of the working surface, considering both positive and negative space.

- Value originality and resist stereotyped concepts.

- Express moods and feelings in personal artwork, using art elements and principles.

- Recognize and use a variety of sources of inspiration and content for the creation of art.

- Plan continuous evaluation and personally complete a work of art.

Use rudimentary perspective that is suitable to various levels of maturity and individual goals.

Demonstrate responsibility in the use and care of art supplies, materials, and equipment.

Discuss the purposes of art, which may be intended to comment upon social practice, celebrate special events, convey private images, materialize beliefs and values, make ideas more understandable.

- Use and evaluate resource materials on art history and appreciations, such as books, periodicals, films, and prints.

- Visit collections of original art in museums, studios, and galleries.

- Research and discuss careers in art. Identify and interview artists in some of these fields.

- Realize that art has a past, that it has changed over time, and that contemporary art is the result of continuous development and change.

- Explain the contributions of artists to society and to the local community.

- Identify the variety of art forms used in business and industry.

- Recognize and value the artistic contributions of one's own cultural heritage as well as those of others.

- Analyze and discuss the ways in which art influences and is influenced by social, political, economic, and technological events.

- Perceive and describe visual forms in terms of both expression and structure.

- Tell how major artistic styles emerged from specific periods and cultures.

- Compare and describe works of art with respect to aesthetic meaning, sensory qualities, style, and materials and processes used to create them.

- Discuss answers to such questions as *What is art?* and *Why is one work of art considered better than another?*

- Make judgments about and show concern for the aesthetic quality of the community environment.

- Integrate experiences in visual arts with creative writing, music, drama, and dance.

- Compare artworks of various styles that depict similar subjects.

- Develop skills of constructive criticism.

- Demonstrate how quality of design affects the functions of products and environments.

- Grow in understanding of and respect for the art expressions of others, including peers and adult artists.

## Books About Artists

Reading biographies of artists will help your students understand the environment in which they lived and the forces that shaped their work. Here are some useful resources.

*Art for Children Series* by Ernest Raboff (Harper & Row)

*Portraits of Women Artists for Children Series* by Robyn Montana Turner (Little, Brown)

*Getting to Know the World's Greatest Artists Series* by Mike Venezia (Children's Press)

> **Art flourishes where there is a sense of adventure.**
>
> —Alfred North Whitehead

## Elements of Art

Help your students sharpen their observation skills and increase their abilities to evaluate and to appreciate works of art by involving them in activities that increase their understanding of the basic elements of art. Here are some ideas.

**Line**—Make a design using different kinds of lines (straight, parallel, wavy, intersecting, and so on).

**Shape**—Split a paper shape in two by cutting across it. Then glue the two pieces onto a sheet of paper, leaving a small space between them.

**Color**—Experiment with shades and tints by painting a picture using only one color.

**Texture**—Make a collage displaying various textures.

**Space**—Cut different sizes of paper all of one shape. Glue the shapes onto a sheet of paper, placing the smaller shapes "behind" the larger ones to suggest distance.

## Works of Art

By giving your students opportunities to study great works of art, you will help them learn about art principles as well as the contributions artists have made to society.

**Obtaining Prints**—Your school district may have prints of paintings, sculptures, and other art forms you may borrow. If such prints are unavailable, look through art books, magazines, or encyclopedias, or search for greeting cards, postcards, or calendars with works of art. Many art museums have outreach programs and other resources for teachers. Call your local museum.

**Asking Questions**—Ask questions to help your students focus on the specific qualities or properties of a work of art. Some questions you could ask follow.

- *Is there any one color that stands out?*
- *What shapes do your see?*
- *What material did the artist use?*
- *What title would you give this piece of work?*
- *What do you think the artist wanted you to think about when you saw his or her work?*

## MUSIC

Whether your school has a designated music teacher or you provide the music program for your class, music instruction in fifth grade should consist of activities designed to develop the following skills.

- Recognize music based on a five tone scale.
- Identify major and minor scales.
- Recognize melodies that have changed key.
- Analyze music written in theme and variation form.
- Understand the form of selected larger compositions.
- Discover the interaction between the elements of music which creates form.
- Differentiate between chords and two or more melodies played together.
- Respond to beautiful tone color that is played or sung.
- Sing songs with changing meters.
- Sing longer phrases in one breath.
- Sing three part rounds and two part songs.
- Sing musically with a loud or soft dynamic level.
- Sing in class with a good blend of tone.
- Develop a repertoire of favorite songs.
- Play major and minor scales in the keys of familiar songs.

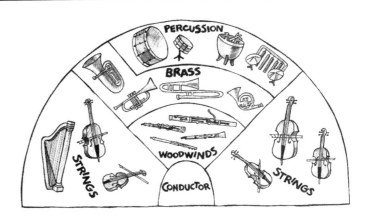

Play intervals from familiar songs on melody bells.

Play a five tone scale.

Perform uneven and syncopated patterns of rhythm in song material.

Play several rhythm patterns in an ensemble using percussion instruments.

Play chords for repeated phrases and accompaniments to three chord songs on the autoharp.

• Discover the various sounds which are produced when individual instruments are played in different ways.

• Select appropriate movements to demonstrate repeated tones, scale patterns, and chord patterns.

• Demonstrate subtle changes of dynamics and tempo.

• Read and write simple chord patterns.

• Differentiate between melody and harmony.

• Identify the expressive characteristics in music of various cultures.

• Create movements that demonstrate polyrhythms.

• Create movements to represent changing and irregular meter and complex rhythms.

• Create movements to represent canons and rounds.

## Sample Activities

### Introduction to the Orchestra

Using the diagram on this page, make a bulletin board display to introduce the sections of the orchestra to your students.

Have students do independent research to find out the answers to the following questions:

What member of the orchestra must always sit to play, even when "The Star-Spangled Banner" is played? (*The cello player*)

The size-pitch relationship is the theory that states the smaller the instrument, the higher the sound; the larger the instrument, the lower the sound. (Except percussion instruments) Using this theory: What instrument sounds the highest in the string family? (*violin*) In the woodwind family? (*flute*) In the brass family? (*trumpet*) What instrument sounds the lowest in the string family? (*double bass*) In the woodwind family? (*bassoon*) In the brass family? (*tuba*)

### Symphony Vocabulary

Students can practice dictionary skills while learning about the symphony by looking up the following vocabulary words:

| | | |
|---|---|---|
| cue | maestro | ovation |
| encore | program | pitch |
| score | baton | composer |
| podium | usher | suite |

**67**

## Music Appreciation Study

You may want to introduce some well-known American composers to your students and explore their music. Some examples are listed below.

### Operas and Musicals

George Gershwin—*Porgy and Bess*

Leonard Bernstein—*West Side Story*

Jerome Kern—*Show Boat*

Richard Rodgers—*Oklahoma, South Pacific, The King & I*

### Band Music

John Philip Sousa—*The Stars and Stripes Forever*

### Folk Music

Woody Guthrie—*This Land Is Your Land*

Pete Seeger—*Where Have All the Flowers Gone?*

### Symphony

Gershwin—*An American in Paris*

> **TIP!**
>
> *Research shows that when children have low self-esteem, the chemicals in their brains shut down pathways in learning situations. Music can change this chemistry and open up those pathways.*

## History and Music

Musical history can be organized in a variety of ways. One way is to divide music into the following six historical periods: Medieval, Renaissance, Baroque, Classical, Romantic, and 20th-Century. Divide the class into six groups and have each group research one of the historical periods. Have the groups make a presentation to the class, which should include samples of music. Most libraries have cassettes and compact discs that may be checked out.

# CHAPTER THREE: ORGANIZATION

## PHYSICAL LAYOUT OF THE CLASSROOM

There are several important issues to consider before you set up your room. Do you share the room? Do you have a self-contained classroom or are the students on a rotational schedule? Notice where the switches and plugs are located. How do you envision the students entering the room? Can you locate your desk in a quiet corner or does it need to be in the front of the class? Do you need a desk? Are you going to use centers? Do you have desks or tables in your room for students? How do you want to arrange student desks—in groups, in rows, or individually? Do you know in advance if any of your students need wheelchair access, or an area where there is little visual distraction? What built-in features like chalkboards, shelves, windows, or sinks will affect where you want students working?

Other important factors that will affect your decisions follow.

- All walkways and high traffic areas should be kept clear for safety. This includes doors, closets, and centers.

- Quiet areas such as the reading corner, the library, the writing, and the poetry centers should be separated from noisy areas, such as the art, the technology, and the music centers.

- The art area should be near a sink for access to water for washing and clean up.

- Certain centers require electricity, such as the computer or the music center. The location of the electric outlets could affect the location of these centers.

- If your classroom computer is going to be on-line, it will have to be close to the phone line.

- Your computer should be located as far as possible from dusty, sunny, and busy places.

- Have separate places in the room for large group activities, small group work, and individual desk areas. You'll also want a large, open area for giving speeches and performing plays and skits.

- You will need places to store student work.

Draw an outline map of you classroom on a large piece of paper. Include any immovable and crucial objects on your classroom "map" such as doors, radiators, posts, electrical outlets, the chalkboard, windows, and bulletin boards. Use small pieces of paper to represent desks, filing cabinets, your computer(s), centers, bookshelves, etc. Make notes on the paper "furniture" of any important things to keep in mind as you are arranging the room on paper such as *needs electricity*. Move things around on the map to get your ideal layout before you move any real furniture.

The desk arrangement you choose should be what works best for you. To facilitate cooperative groups, four of five students to a table cluster works nicely for a group.

The top area of bookshelves can be used for globes, portfolio cases, a homework bin, and parent communication folders. Plastic crates that hold hanging files are very useful. Place wastebaskets strategically around the room. Have a file cabinet ready to use for all subjects. Take your time to think the room arrangement through ahead of time. As the year develops, change it according to your needs.

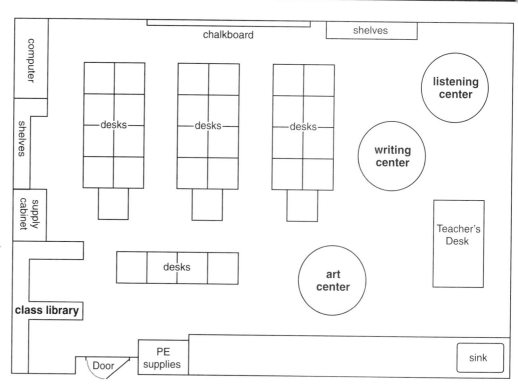

# SCHEDULING

Following a daily schedule will make you more effective as a teacher. Schedules let the students know what is coming next, and keep you on track. To make a schedule, start by finding out what times may be planned for you already. Your school may have music, art, or science programs that regularly require students to be away from your classroom. Your principal may want to have students who are in an English Language Development Program to be meeting at the same time. There are usually scheduled recess or lunch times. You may have scheduled yard, bus, or lunchroom duties.

Once you know when students will be with you, divide the day into blocks of time for each subject. Opportunities to read, write, and work with mathematics should occur every day. Your school or district may have requirements about the minimal amount of time that should be devoted to certain subjects. If you have an assistant, consider how you will use her or him during the time assigned to you.

> Any subject can be effectively taught in some intellectually honest form to any child at any stage of development.
>
> —Jerome Bruner, <u>The Process of Education</u>, 1960

Another important consideration to keep in mind as you develop a class schedule is that your fifth-graders will probably be more focused in the morning than in the afternoon. You might want to schedule activities that require more concentration in the morning.

Many teachers write their schedule on a posterboard and post in the class. Others prefer to write it on the board so that students get in the habit of consulting it every day. If it is written on a chalkboard or easel pad every day, writing it can become a student job. A sample schedule is in the sidebar.

## The Entry Task

Assigning an entry task is a great way to start out the day. Post a different task on the chalkboard every day. Suggested entry tasks are journal entries in science, writing, personal, or math journals, or a logic problem. When students arrive, they check the task notice. This allows students some time to make the transition from home, morning care, or school bus to class. Frequently, students arrive at school after being rushed every moment since they woke up. An entry task helps the students settle and focus, and gives you time for last-minute preparations or to handle any last-minute crisis.

## Opening

Possible activities for the opening of the day include the flag salute, taking attendance, reviewing and updating the calendar, introduction of theme activities, presentation of activities planned for the day, and collecting homework. Establish a regular routine for the opening. It can set the tone for the day. Interact and observe your students as you go through the activities. You will quickly learn to spot who is having a hard day and may need some encouragement to get on track.

## Closing

Use the last 15 minutes of the day to bring your class together for a group seated activity. You can use this time to summarize the day with a closing activity such as the *Activity Review Cards* (description follows), review the homework assignment for the evening, remind students of any special events of the next day, or to pass out special recognitions you would like to give. Your students will benefit by having a few moments of mental regrouping before they have to go home, go to day care, or get on a bus. You will benefit by taking an opportunity to assess the instructional day with your students and having a relatively calm end of the day.

### Sample Daily Schedule

**School Day 8:00–2:30**

|  |  |
| --- | --- |
| 8:00 | Entry Task |
| 8:15 | Opening |
| 8:50 | Math |
| 9:30 | Recess |
| 9:45 | Reading |
| | Full Group Instruction/ Conferences/ Independent Work/ Centers |
| 10:55 | Spelling |
| 11:10 | Lunch |
| 11:55 | Sustained Silent Reading |
| 12:10 | Writer's Workshop (Mon., Wed.) |
| | Science/ Social Studies (Tues., Thurs.) |
| | Art (Fri.) |
| 1:15 | Recess |
| 1:25 | Physical Education (Mon., Wed., Fri.) |
| | Music/ Computer Lab (Tues., Thurs.) |
| 2:15 | Closing |
| 2:30 | Dismissal |

**71**

### Activity Review Cards

As part of your closing activities, review the lessons and activities of the day as a group. As students tell you what happened during the day, you write it onto a 5" x 7" index card with the day's date at the top. Display the index cards in a calendar-like display, adding to the display for the month. At the end of the month, bind the cards into a class book for the classroom library. You will all enjoy rereading the activity books at different points in the year. An additional benefit is that you will have an instant assessment of what parts of your instructional day were most effective.

# TRANSITIONS

Any time you change activities, you present your students with problems to solve. They need to stop what they are doing, put it away, and move to the next activity. This is a challenge for some students. You will notice that most students are not their quietest while in transition. You can reduce the stress of transition time by having reasonable expectations of your students, and explaining what the expectations are in advance. First, you need to get their attention.

Many teachers pick a signal to attract students' attention. Commonly used signals include ringing a small bell, turning out the lights, clapping, or

holding one hand in the air. Do not give an instructions until you have the attention of al your students. Once you have their attention, giv them the following information.

- Explain what is going to happen.

- Indicate how they will move such as by forming a line or walking across the room.

- Tell them where they will be going.

- Inform them what they will be doing.

> ### TIP!
>
> *Do you know why you do what you do in your classroom? Can you explain it?*

Moving students from place to place, either within a classroom or from the classroom to another location at the school can be tricky. Some schools require that students move from place to place in single file, while other schools do not regiment this movement. If you are new to your school, consult colleagues to find out what your school culture is like.

# RECORD KEEPING AND ORGANIZATION

The key to a successful classroom is being organized. Know what records your school requires, and what records your teaching plans require. Records you may need to keep include aily attendance records, assessment records ncluding portfolios and test results), lesson lans, permanent school records (usually kept at chool), homework tracking, and reading logs. lan your record keeping as soon as you know you ave a class.

## Number

When you get your class list, ssign each student a number. tudents place this number on ll of their work next to their name. When checking for missing work, put the work in numerical order and scan the numbers to find who has turned work in. The numbers can also be used to count off when lining up or collecting work. The number system is particularly useful if your class size changes a lot during the year. You ust give new students the next number or reassign a number belonging to a former student who has moved.

## Grade Book

Daily assignments can be recorded in a grade book. Abbreviations are useful because grade books generally have small spaces to write in and they take less time to write on students' papers. You may want to post your specific abbreviations for your students to refer to. A sample follows.

✓ = assignment received

I = incomplete

L = late

AB = absent

EX = excused

> **Teaching is an instinctual art, mindful of potential, craving of realizations, a pausing, seamless process.**
>
> —A Bartlett Giamatti, "The American Teacher," _Harper's_, July 1980.

**TIP!**

_Make a "to do" list at the beginning of each week. Add items each day as they come up. Check off items as you do them._

An empty box with a circle in it signifies that the assignment is missing. At the end of the grading period an effort grade can be determined by comparing the number of assignments to the number of completions.

## Attendance

Attendance recording policy is usually set by the school. Make notations of absences, late arrivals, and early dismissals on your desk calendar, in your plan book, or in your grade book. These notes help to verify office records and will need to be recorded on report cards.

## Collecting Work

Establish a regular routine for turning in papers. Some teachers like to have bins where students place their work. Others like to have monitors collect assignments from their tables/rows. Choose a method that you feel comfortable with.

## Plan Book

Reduce the amount of time you spend preparing for lessons by color-coding your plans. Use a different color of pen for each task that needs to be completed before a lesson. For example, use a blue pen to note all the pages that need to be reproduced for an entire day or week. This way you will be able to do all the reproducing at one time. If you use a red pen to write down all the titles of books you want to borrow from the library, you will be able to take a quick look and check out all the books at one time. Write in green all the supplies you need to gather.

## Theme Boxes

Collect boxes and use them for storing all of the materials you need for a particular unit. For example, you might include related literature books, samples of projects, reproducible pages, and index cards with ideas for activities written on them. Remember to label the outsides of the boxes with the names of the themes.

## Timesavers

Reduce the time you spend on nonteaching tasks with these shortcuts, and you'll find that you have more time to devote to teaching.

**Bulletin Boards**—Use neutral colors that can be used all year long for your bulletin board backgrounds. Just change the borders if you want them to correspond to a particular theme or season.

**Frequent Forms**—Make copies of notes that you frequently write to parents, the school office, the school nurse, and others.

**Student Involvement**—Let your students help you with many classroom chores. They can help pass out materials, sharpen pencils, empty trash, take care of class pets, check games for lost pieces, check-in homework, and many other tasks.

# ASSESSMENT

The purpose of assessment is to gain better information about each student, such as what he or she has learned, the way that he or she learned it, and how he or she uses what was learned. The information you get from assessments can be used to help you plan future instruction for your students. Explanations of some different kinds of assessments follow. Choose the ones that work best for each particular situation.

## Portfolios

Portfolios can be used as a form of assessment to show student achievement. A portfolio is a long-term record of student progress, and should include samples of work selected by you, samples selected by the student, and self-evaluations written by the student. They will help you see a clear and understandable picture that provides more information about what a student knows than a test score does. It allows you to identify and recognize different learning styles among your students, and to include students an active role in the assessment process.

You may want to include the following in the portfolios:

**Math**
- Samples of student-created word problems

- Photographs showing the students using math manipulatives to solve problems

- Samples of work related to the same math concept from different times of the school year

- The students' written explanations about a math concept such as ratios

**Writing**
- Writing samples in different stages of the writing process

Several writing samples collected at different times of the year

Samples of different kinds of writing such as essays, poems, and reports

A piece of writing that the student feels is his or her best work with an explanation of why the piece was selected

### Science
Photographs of the students doing science experiments

Diagrams drawn by the students

Observations and logs written by the students

### Social Studies
Notes from research on the life of a historical figure

Time lines

Maps

## Interview Assessment

Interviews are a way to see a student's true level of understanding. Often a student has memorized an answer or a fact but doesn't understand the concept. For example, in math, if you want to see if a student knows how to divide, instead of having him or her write an answer to a problem, ask him or her to give an example of a real-life situation where division would be used.

## Performance Assessment

The purpose of performance assessments is to look at how students are working, as well as at the completed tasks or products. For example, a student who constructs a compass is assessed on how he or she makes the compass and his or her understanding of how a compass works, rather than the answers on a test about magnetism. There are many benefits to using performance assessment. With performance assessments you will be able to see:

- Reasoning—Does the student reason soundly and raise questions?

- Concentration—Does the student concentrate and work independently?

- Flexibility—Does the student change strategies when one doesn't work?

- Cooperation—Does the student work well with others?

- Communication—Does the student communicate through discussing, writing, and explaining his or her ideas?

# REPORT CARDS

As you figure grades for report cards, you will probably be able to use your best judgment about what work should be reflected in the final grade and what can be given greater or lesser importance. Before you sit down to write your report cards, gather all relevant material—portfolios, your grade book, and anecdotal records. Expect to spend a week or two doing report cards. Some schools and districts provide pre-printed report card forms that you fill in. Others will provide you with blank forms on which to hand write grades that become the permanent report card. It can be useful to make copies of your blank forms—one for each student. You can compile your records on this sheet, and so that any mistakes you make (and you will make some) will be on a non-permanent record which you can then copy.

What are the important grades to include in this reporting period? Some schools and districts will mandate some reporting. Others will leave it to your professional judgment. Is every grade as important as the others? Some teachers like to drop the worst grade from the student's work and then average the rest of the grades. Others like to weight different work differently to reflect their curricular goals. For example, if a teacher feels that

> **In teaching you cannot see the fruit of a day's work. It is invisible and remains so, maybe for twenty years.**
> —Jacques Barzun, <u>Teacher in America</u>, 1944

# STANDARDIZED TESTS

Standardized tests and other written tests still hav a role in assessing student learning. There ar times when measuring a child to an establishe standard is necessary, however, a test is only on piece of information about a child. Your schoo district or state will probably require that you students take a standardized test at one poin during the year. Testing can sometimes last for whole week.

Before beginning these tests, talk to the student about the testing process. Sharing their thought can help relieve some of their anxieties abou standardized tests. Brainstorm test-takin strategies and give tips. Provide a calm anc relaxing environment. Check the temperature o the room, and the lighting beforehand so there' time to make any necessary adjustments. Reduce or cancel homework assignments during the testing period. Remind parents that testing time is approaching and ask that they please make sure that their children:

process-oriented projects (like writing a short story) is more important than performance on a fill-in-the-blank test, he or she may choose to consider performance on the project to be worth 90% of the grade, and performance on the test to be worth 10%.

Many report cards have sections for teacher comments. Draft your comments on a separate sheet of paper before you write them on the final document. Edit your comments for content and mechanical errors. Use a positive tone when writing report cards. If a student has done an exceptional project or shows excellence in any academic, recreational, or social area, mention it. Your words will be remembered for many years.

## TIP!

*Remember, quickest does not equal most talented. The purpose of time in standardized tests is solely to create a "normal distribution."*

1. Get a good night's rest.

2. Eat a nutritious breakfast and bring a snack for break time.

3. Arrive at school on time.

Make a "Do Not Disturb— Testing Zone" sign to put on the door before beginning each testing session. Have extra pencils ready to use. During the actual testing periods, make sure that everyone is working on the correct page. During breaks, lead the class in stretching exercises. Even just dropping your arms and shaking your hands helps relax those tense muscles. Each day after the testing session is over, set aside time for the class to have a free recess. Fifth graders still need to move around a lot and sometimes the hardest part of testing is just having to sit still for a required length of time.

FS122007 Getting Ready to Teach Fifth Grade

# CHAPTER FOUR: RELATIONSHIPS

## DISCIPLINE

By taking the time to manage student behavior effectively, you will find that you have a classroom that runs smoothly and facilitates learning. Empower yourself with these practical tips and positive ideas.

### Establishing Rules

Build a foundation for behavior management by specifying your classroom rules along with their consequences and rewards. Post your rules in a location that is always visible. Keep the rules simple and limit them to four or five. Involve students in brainstorming a list of rules that will help everyone work successfully in class. Then work together to combine and condense the list to a few of the most important rules and keep them

posted in the classroom. Use rules that describe the behaviors you want instead of listing things the students cannot do. *Respect the rights and property of others* is a positive way of saying *Don't take things that belong to others.* Refer to the rules as expectations. Let your students know this is how you expect them to behave. Once the rules are established, they need to be enforced consistently. Make students aware that they are responsible for their behavior. When a rule is broken, always implement a consequence. Pick a consequence that is fair and logical, and deliver it right away. This way your students will learn that you are a person of your word, that there is order in your classroom, and that you expect them to follow the rules.

### Get Their Attention

Start any lesson or activity only when you have everyone's attention. If you try teaching while some students are inattentive, your students will get the idea that it is permissible to talk while you are teaching.

## Monitoring

Circulate around the room about two minutes after the students have started a written assignment. Check to see that each student has started and provide individual instruction as needed. This personal and positive attention will help students work more effectively.

## Do As I Do

You provide the best example for your students' behavior. You provide a positive example for your students by being courteous, in control, patient, and organized. If you want your students to use quiet voices in the classroom, then you should use a quiet voice as you move around the room. "Do as I say, not as I do" teachers send mixed messages that confuse student and invite misbehavior.

## Time Out

A time-out period for students who break the rules can be effective because it sends a message that when behavior is inappropriate there is a consequence for the behavior. Pick a spot in the classroom where a student can be isolated, yet still be directly supervised by you. Decide what behaviors will merit an immediate time-out. Include students in making this decision. When sending a student to the time-out area, do not shame, blame, discuss, or lecture. As soon as the behavior starts, simply state the behavior and the consequence in a matter-of-fact fashion. Set a timer for the number of minutes for the time-out. Keep in mind that when the time-out is over, the incident is over. Let go of your feelings about the behavior and welcome the student back into the group.

## Positive Reinforcement

Positive rewards can be effective motivators and can reinforce appropriate behavior in your students. Here is one example of a positive reward. Put an empty glass jar in the front of the classroom.

> ### TIP!
>
> *Students can let off steam by exercising, pounding clay, singing loudly, laughing, and dancing and jumping to music. Calming activities include stretching to soothing music and sensory experiences such as stroking the class pet, doing an art project, or listening to quiet music.*

Whenever all students are behaving appropriately drop a few kernels of unpopped popcorn into the jar. When the jar is full, pop the popcorn and have a class popcorn party.

## Assertive Techniques

These techniques will help prevent students from interfering with the learning of others.

**Soft Voice**—When disciplining a student, deliver your words in a soft, even-paced tone.

**Give "I" Messages**—Be firm and specific, but accepting. Give clear descriptions of what is expected. Say *I want you to* (state the positive behavior). Try to avoid statements that focus on the misbehavior such as *I want you to stop.* These type of statements usually trigger confrontation and denial.

**Eye Contact**—Walk over to the student, look him or her in the eyes, and deliver your message about the behavior. Maintain eye contact for a moment afterward.

**Keep Calm**—If you feel upset over a student's behavior, postpone taking any action. Deal with the student later, when you feel more calm. This helps you to effectively cope with the situation and it models a nonaggressive approach to communication.

## Settling Disputes

Encourage students involved in a disagreement to settle their own arguments, but be available to guide the problem-solving process. By allowing students to handle problems for themselves, they learn to rely on themselves and not on you.

Facilitate problem-solving by teaching your students conflict resolution. Some situations may warrant a cooling-off period beforehand. Once all parties involved are ready, use these five steps to help the students stay focused on the problem and the process.

1. **Gather facts**—Allow each person a chance to tell what happened and how he or she feels about what happened. As the negotiator, you need to remain neutral. Try not to display any negative feelings or lay blame on anyone. Dialogue using phrases such as: "What happened?" and "How did you feel when . . .?"

2. **State the problem**—Name the general problem so that it expresses everyone's needs. *Jake, you want _____, and Katie, you want _____.* The problem may need to be reworded several times before full agreement is reached.

3. **Solve the Problem**—Ask the involved students to think of ways to solve the problem. Encourage each person to create ideas to help settle the matter. You may want them to write these ideas down. Ask questions such as *What can you do so that everyone will be happy? What can you do to meet everyone's needs?*

4. **Evaluation**—Have students evaluate the ideas and determine the consequence of each choice. Have them decide which solution could make both parties happy.

5. **Make a Plan**—Have the students write out an agreement stating how the problem will be solved. Meet with the students to see if the solution was successful. At that time determine whether a new agreement is needed.

# SOCIAL ORDER OF THE ROOM

Help your students develop responsibility by giving them jobs in the classroom. If you rotate the jobs weekly, the students will get more chances to do each job. One way to set up the jobs is with a government theme by using titles of government jobs in Washington D.C. These are some examples of jobs and duties:

> **We have one simple rule here: Be kind.**
>
> **—Sam Jaffe, Lost Horizon, 1937**

**Class President**—This person presides over the opening procedures.

**Vice President**—This person fills in when the president is absent.

**Chief Justice**—This person presides over classroom meetings.

**Treasurer**—This person is responsible for taking the lunch count.

**Defense Secretary**—This person is responsible for class safety drills.

**Secretary of the Interior**—This person is responsible for school and yard equipment.

**Secretary of Agriculture**—This person is responsible for the class plants.

**Secretary of Commerce**—This person is responsible for computers, video equipment, etc.

**Secretary of Transportation**—This person is a line leader.

**Secretary of Energy**—This person is responsible for the lights.

**Secretary of the Environment**—This person is in charge of room clean up.

**Librarian of Congress**—This person is responsible for maintaining classroom library books.

Create other job titles and add assistants if you want everyone to have a job each week.

# THE SCHOOL COMMUNITY

Many people comprise the school. Getting to know each one can be a difficult task, however, it is well worth it. Knowing the people to whom you can go for support makes life at school easier.

## Principal

Usually the principal of a school is a former teacher who has gone to school to get an administrative credential. In many schools and districts, the principal is the person who hires you at a school, while the school district employs you.

The principal is your manager. He or she is accountable to the powers-that-be and to parents for what occurs in your classroom. Some principals spend a lot of time being educational leaders—keeping in touch with teachers and students, spending time in the classroom and in the community areas like the playground or lunchroom. Other principals focus their energies on running the business side of the school. Their jobs are defined in part by the system in which they work.

As your manager, your principal will observe your work in the classroom. He or she may make an appointment with you to see a lesson or may drop in to see what you do in the classroom. Formal and informal observations can be valuable learning experiences for you.

### TIP!

*Take the time to get to know the people with whom you work. You will not only form friendships, but you'll build a support system as well.*

You will want to communicate well with your principal. To communicate well, you must share your frustrations and your successes. When you have questions or difficulty dealing with a parent, part of the principal's job is to support you. Don't forget to share your successes with your principal. He or she will be happy to hear those, too!

### Buddy Teacher

Find a teacher at your grade level to whom you feel comfortable asking everyday questions about anything. A buddy teacher will let you know about school culture. Questions will come up about core literature books, curriculum planning, field trips, assemblies, and more, specific to your grade level. A buddy teacher might just have the answer to your question.

### Colleagues

On one hand, teaching is isolating. You spend most of your days with people much younger than you are, and frequently you will feel alone dealing with the challenges in your classroom, because you are alone. You can alleviate this feeling by

getting to know the people with whom you work. Many schools have an area where you can eat lunch or meet with other teachers. Find common interests to discuss besides work. Frequently teachers at a school will have a social committee to plan gatherings and special events. Try to participate in as many as possible. A natural outgrowth of the friendships you build is a support system.

### Custodian

Get to know the custodian(s) of the school. They know where everything is. When you need furniture, special cleaning tools, light bulbs, and paper towels, talk to a custodian. Teach students to be responsible for cleaning the classroom at the end of the day. This will make the custodian's job a lot easier, and create an ally for you. There will come the day that your students have had a big party, you have been painting, several students drop paint water on the floor, and you will need special help cleaning.

Know how to request supplies such as tissues and paper towels. Learn how to request repairs, verbally or in writing if you need them. Sometimes you need to submit a work order through the office.

## Office Manager

The people who run the office keep the school moving. This is a tremendous job. Every piece of paper that comes to the school goes through the office. Attendance, payroll, mail, bulletins, field trip requests, book orders, and all official outward bound papers are handled by the front office. Ask questions and get familiar with the procedures. Find out about deadlines for field trip requests, district mail, and other information from the front office.

## Supply Manager

Learn what supplies are available on site and how to obtain them. There also may be a list of materials. Sometimes, you will need to place an order well in advance. While you are planning, make a list of supplies you will need. Place your order in time to get the supplies and materials you need for your classroom.

## Resource Teachers

Many schools have teachers who do not have their own classrooms. They may provide special services such as a reading laboratory, coordinate the art or music programs, or manage the instructional materials owned by the school. Frequently, resource teachers will be able to answer questions or make suggestions about educational and classroom management issues. In some schools where the principal is extremely busy, the resource teacher is the first person you ask for educational program support.

Some school districts maintain centralized resource centers for teachers where you may have access to free photocopying services and educational materials. The principal or resource teacher will know whether such a place exists, where it is, and how to use it.

## Librarian

The school librarian can be another strong resource for you. Frequently, school libraries have a regularly scheduled time when your students will go to the library to learn about resources there, enjoy literacy activities, read, and check out books.

> We might cease thinking of school as a place, and learn to believe that it is basically relationships between children and adults, and between children and other children. The four walls and the principal's office would cease to loom so hugely as the essential ingredients.
>
> —George Dennison, The Lives of Children, 1969

The school librarian knows what books are in the library and can help you find literature and nonfiction that will support your program.

## School Nurse

Many schools and districts have a school nurse full- or part-time. The nurse will coordinate hearing and vision screenings, keep medical information on students with health problems, and often has an office with beds where students who have taken ill can lie down. If you are concerned about a student"s health, consult the nurse. He or she many also be able to help you find resources to assist the families of your students who need health care services.

## The Teacher's Union

Many public school district teachers are represented by a union. Usually, there will be at least one union representative at your school. Particularly in a large district, a union representative can be helpful in learning who you have to speak to for help in employment issues.

## PTA

The PTA is an organization of parents and teachers united to work together to improve the school. The PTA is different in every school. some are active, some are not. Some will want you to be active in their organization, some will not. Most PTA's raise funds for special projects that the school has identified as necessary or wanted. Find out what activities the PTA handles at your school. They may have a project that interests you or could directly benefit your class.

# HOME/SCHOOL CONNECTION

Make parents valuable resources in your classroom by establishing and maintaining open lines of communication and by letting them take active roles in their children's learning. The more parents know about what is happening at school, the more likely it is that they will be supportive and involved.

### Back to School Night

Most schools hold a Back-to-School or Parent Night soon after the school year begins. This evening program gives parents an opportunity to meet you and learn about what their children will be doing in fifth grade. This is the best time to inform parents about the curriculum and to lay the foundation for good communication between home and school.

> ## TIP!
> *Select a few students each week and call their parents to give a brief update on their progress.*

Before this event, you'll want to write and make copies of a fact sheet. The fact sheet should explain the school year in a nutshell. Inform parents when and how you are available for phone calls and conferences. Ask that parents inform you of anything out of the ordinary that is affecting their child such as death of a loved one; hospitalization of a parent; out-of-town parents; a divorce. Let them know that you want them to share their concerns and questions with you. If you all work together, this year will be successful and enjoyable. Include information such as classroom rules, discipline procedures, homework policy, birthday celebration policy, daily and/or weekly schedule, ways parents can help, and an explanation of teaching strategies you'll be using. Send fact sheets home to those families who were unable to attend.

To prepare for the event, have students clean the classroom and write welcome letters to thank their parents for attending. Use construction paper folded in half and have the students write their parents names on the outside of the note. This way the notes can also be used as a name card to help parents find where they sit that evening. Let students choose some favorite pieces of work to display. It is a good idea to leave off grades so that parents don't make comparisons. Label classroom work areas with an explanation about what the students do in each area. Take photos of your students involved in daily activities. Share the photos to give parents a good indication of what a typical day is like.

Arrive early so that you can check on everything before your guests arrive. Greet everyone at the front door with a smile and a handshake. Have parents sign in by name and their child's name. Briefly explain the most important items found in the fact sheet and explain your expectations for the year. Display textbooks and other learning materials. Ask for parent volunteers and pass around a sign up sheet with specific requests.

f possible, introduce your homeroom parent, room assistant, or any other special aides. Have a question and answer session for general questions only. Remind parents that this is not a night for individual conferences, but is an informational session about your classroom. Any specific or personal questions can be dealt with later at a conference. Remind them that you are available for conferences during regular school hours. You might want to have parents write their child a short note and leave it in his or her desk. The students will love finding the notes the next day.

## Newsletter

Weekly newsletters help keep the parents informed on what's going on in the classroom and what important events are coming up. Include dates of upcoming events, due dates for student assignments, and any supplies parents can send in to help your class. You might even get the students involved in producing the newsletter.

## Parent-Teacher Conferences

Parent-teacher conferences provide opportunities for parents and teachers to focus on an individual student's learning experiences. During a conference, academic progress, work habits, social skills, and special talents can be discussed face-to-face, and joint plans for improvement can be made. Include these strategies for effective parent conferences:

**Mini-Conference**—Have a mini conference with each student beforehand. Discuss areas of strength, areas for growth, and areas of concern. This procedure helps to relieve their stress. You may even want to invite students to attend their conference with their parents.

**Scheduling**—Schedule conferences carefully. Allow enough time to talk to each parent without rushing. Post your schedule outside your door. Stick to the schedule and tell parents who arrive late or those whose conferences exceed the given time to reschedule for another time.

**Establish Rapport**—Sit beside parents rather than across a table. This makes them feel more comfortable.

**Stress the Positive**—Remember to always give some positive comments about each student. If you need to inform parents about weaknesses, use positive words and phrases to get your message across and offer suggestions for improvement.

**Assure Privacy**—Keep your conversations private. Be sure no other adults or students are able to overhear what you are saying.

## Student Folders

Print each student's name and number on the outside of a manila folder and keep the folders in numerical order in a file box. As papers are graded, they can be filed in student folders. Establish a weekly routine for students to take their folder home and return it the following day. Let the parents know which day to expect the folder and then request that they sign it or write their initials to indicate that it arrived home safely.

## Resource Library

Set up a parent resource library in your classroom. Include books about effective parenting and games and learning activities that parents can use with their children at home. Invite parents to check out the resources and ask willing parents to write reviews for the class newsletter about what they checked out.

> **I never before understood the depth of gratitude a parent can feel for a teacher who creates a classroom environment that enables children to love learning, to exhibit genuine enthusiasm and excitement for purposeful and meaningful tasks, and to a new community of friends.**
>
> —Irene Hannigan, Off to School—A Parent's-Eye View of the Kindergarten Year (NAEYC, 1998)

**83**

### Open House

This is usually a longer and more elaborate event than Back-to-School night. This is generally held towards the end of the school year and students attend with their parents, grandparents, and other important people in their lives. It's a time for the students to show off! Your classroom and the students' efforts for the year are on display. It is a good idea to start planning projects for this event before the school year begins. You may want to save an example of each class project by inviting a student to make a second one for you to keep for Open House. Have students select their best efforts to display in their portfolios. Books published by the class, classroom newsletters, state reports, science experiments, geography projects, picture posters, are all items that make good visuals. If you have access to a VCR, you can show video tapes of classroom skits and presentations. Ask students to introduce you to their guests that evening. Let your students know that they are responsible for acting as classroom ambassadors at Open House by escorting their guests and showing them around the classroom.

# HOMEWORK

Homework is an important part of your students' development. It should be used to reinforce concepts taught at school, help develop lifelong study habits, and to communicate to parents about the curriculum. At the beginning of the year, communicate your expectations about homework to both the students and their parents. Establish general guidelines such as when homework is due, grading policies, and if late homework will be accepted. Here are some tips you can give to parents about how they can help to make the most of the homework experience.

- Make homework rules together with your child.

- Provide a quiet place for your child to do homework. Make sure there is sufficient light and distractions are kept to a minimum.

- Show an interest in your child's homework and ask about it each night. Encourage your child

to work independently, but give assistance when needed.

- Give your child a healthy snack before doing homework. This should help with concentration.

- Give lots of positive words of encouragement.

# CLASSROOM VOLUNTEERS

There are many ways that you can use volunteers in your classroom. Volunteers can be parents, grandparents, and adult siblings. Some volunteers may be able to help on a regular basis, others may be able to help for special projects or field trips. Others may be able to help you prepare materials at home.

You can begin recruiting volunteers at Back-to-School night. Once you've enlisted a group of volunteers, you may want to hold a special training workshop. At this time you can discuss relevant classroom procedures and show your volunteers how to operate various pieces of equipment, such as the copier, the laminating machine, and the overhead projector. At the end of the year, you might want to hold a special recognition reception to recognize the efforts made by your volunteers. Volunteers can lighten your load. Let them help you in any way they can. Here are a few examples.

**Classroom Help**—You may want to have volunteers work in the classroom with individual students who need help, or with small group activities.

**Help at Home**—Volunteers can help you prepare materials. For example, if you are planning a bulletin board display about famous composers and you wanted lots of musical note shapes cut out, a volunteer could do that for you at home.

**Special Speakers**—Invite parents to share their talents or expertise with the class. They can speak about their careers, demonstrate a hobby, discuss a trip or vacation, share a favorite book, or teach an art project. Schedule these visits throughout the year.

**Donations**—Don't be shy about asking for things you need or want for the class. Just ask in advance and be specific about what you want. (Example: a bag of potatoes for a cooking project.) Send a thank you note.

**Chaperones**—Volunteers can accompany the class on field trips. The number of chaperones you will need varies from trip to trip. Some sites require a certain number of adults while others limit the number allowed. Arrange for these volunteers as far in advance as possible. Divide the students into groups and assign a chaperone to each group. Give each chaperone an index card with the names of the students in their group, an approximate schedule for the day, and a list of student-behavior expectations. If possible, don't assign yourself to a group. This allows you to check in on each group and permits you to personally escort any student who needs special attention.

# STARTING THE YEAR

The first days of school set the tone for the entire year. You want to get to know each other and establish classroom routines and procedures. The following ideas and activities can be used to help students feel more comfortable during the first days of school.

**Fascinating Facts**—Ask each student to write down one interesting thing about himself or herself and turn it in. Have all students stand up. Read the facts aloud one at a time. Give students three chances to guess who the fact is about. If the student is guessed, then he or she may

> Education in the long run is an affair that works itself out between the individual student and his opportunities. Methods of which we talk so much play but a minor part. Offer the opportunities, leave the student to his natural reaction on them, and he will work out his personal destiny, be it a high one or a low one.
>
> —William James, speech, Stanford's Ideal Destiny, Stanford University, 1906

sit down. By process of elimination, all students will eventually be guessed.

**Class Stars**—Make up a large star for each student and write his or her name on it. Decorate the front door with these. As the students enter the class have them remove their stars and take them to their desks. Ask them to add their birthdates and decorate the stars. Then make a class time line and have each student place his or her star in the appropriate place.

**Name Circle**—Once everyone has been introduced, stand in a circle. You start the game by giving your name. The person next to you repeats your name and then says his or her name. This rename and name pattern continues all the way around the circle. Once you've reached the end, see if anyone can name every person in the circle. Allow everyone who wants a chance to try this.

**Word Search**—Have a large word-search poster taped on the front board. Use the class roster to write out names on a piece of poster board divided into one-inch squares. Intersect as many names as possible. Then fill in the empty spaces with letters of the alphabet. Ask students to find their names and circle them.

**TIP!**

*Periodically, send thank you notes to your volunteers to let them know how appreciated they truly are.*

**85**

**Dear Teacher**—Since there isn't time to sit down and get to know every student during the first few days, you might want to have the students each write a letter introducing themselves to you. Encourage students to tell about their likes and dislikes, their families, their favorite subjects and topics, and what they hope to do in school this year.

**Interview the Teacher**—Your students will love the opportunity to get to know you. Hold an interview session and allow the students to ask you questions. They may want to ask you about your childhood, your family, your hobbies, and so on.

# ENDING THE YEAR

Before you know it, the school year will be coming to an end. The end of the year is an exciting as well as an exhausting time. Plan activities that let students reflect on the past year and look forward to the next. You may want to try these.

**Photo Posters**—This is an on-going project that culminates at the end of the year. Every month take a close up picture of each student. Pictures should be highlights of fifth grade. Include the first day of school, special projects, and performances. Keep developed pictures filed in individual student envelopes and store all of them in a box for safekeeping. Let each student arrange his or her photos on a large piece of poster board and glue them in place. Let the students use the creative ideas to decorate the posters.

**Next Grade Interviews**—Ask a sixth-grade teacher to allow a group of his or her students to visit your classroom so that your students can interview them about what it is like in sixth grade. If your students are going to middle school next year, find a teacher at the middle school who would be willing to help you out. Have your students write their questions. Then compile the questions and send them to the teacher at the middle school. Ask the teacher to have some of his or her students answer the questions and send them to your class.

**Dear New Student**—Have your students write letters of advice to the students who will be in your class next year. Have them explain what fifth grade is like and give tips for how to do well. Then share the letters with your new students at the beginning of the next year.

## TIP!

*Students will feel more comfortable about making mistakes if they realize it happens to everyone. Take the time to share some of your experiences with your students.*

# CHAPTER FIVE: CLOSING THOUGHTS

## ENGLISH LANGUAGE DEVELOPMENT

You may have students in your class who do not speak English as a first language. In schools where there are many students who speak languages other than English as a first language, you will probably have access to an English Language Development program with guidelines for its use outlined by your school or district. Remember, learning a language is a process. It took you years to speak English well, and you were probably able to concentrate most of your language development on one language.

If you find yourself with a small group of non-English speaking students in your class, and you have no administrative support, check your school's resource room, local university library, or Internet resources for some specific plans and courses of study to assist the students. Some quick guidelines include providing picture cues for certain activities. Teach students the names of the activities and materials (in the context of doing the activity) so that when they hear or see those words they will know what books or materials they need.

Assign the students peer mentors who can help them learn classroom vocabulary. When you change activities, take a moment to approach your non-English speaking students, look at them, and speak at a slower rate using a simple language structure with instructions. Model appropriate responses to questions.

**87**

## Special Education Terms

**Mainstreaming**—Placing a student with disabilities in a regular education classroom.

**IDEA**—*Individuals with Disabilities Education Act,* passed in 1990. IDEA guarantees a student with disabilities the right to a free and appropriate education in the least restrictive environment, with maximum support of mainstreaming. Special classes are used only when appropriate to meet the needs of the individual student.

**Least Restrictive Environment**—The regular classroom setting. A child may be removed from the regular classroom when the disability is such that the education in regular classes cannot be achieved satisfactorily. For example, a child with a reading disability may appropriately be educated in most academic areas in the regular classroom with assistance, but may need to be removed from the regular classroom to work one-one-one in the area of reading.

**Most Restrictive Environment**—Complete removal from mainstream society, such as an institution or hospital setting.

**IEP**—The *Individualized Education Program* required for each student receiving special education.

Your non-English speaking students also come from cultures where acceptable body language differs from what you may be used to. Perhaps as a child you were raised to look at an adult when the adult was talking to you. Looking away was disrespectful. Many cultures consider a child who looks an adult in the face insolent and defiant, so a well-mannered child will never look at an adult directly. Increase your level of awareness of the body language of these students.

Include the students in activities. Model respect for their cultures and their intelligence to the class. Set the tone for acceptance of these students in your class. Your students will follow you. What to you may be little acts of kindness may shine out as beacons of goodwill and inspiration to the student struggling to understand a new language and a new culture.

# MAINSTREAMING

If you are the teacher of a student on an IEP, you are responsible for implementing the curriculum to fulfill the goals and objectives. However, you are not in this alone. Members of the IEP team should work closely with you. Help is available if you ask. Team members include the school nurse, the special education teacher, the school psychologist, a behavioral consultant, an occupational therapist, a special education supervisor, and other school personnel. The IEP team meets annually to discuss goals and objectives and to make sure that progress is being made.

Students with special needs can be successful in the regular education classroom. Be receptive to and accommodate their individual needs.

# BUILDING SELF-ESTEEM

By planning activities that promote confidence in' oneself, you will enhance academic growth. Try some of these ideas.

## Caught You

Let your students participate in building one another's self-esteem. Have them keep a look out for classmates who exhibit positive behaviors, such as voluntarily helping a student who needs it, cleaning up the classroom, or sharing. When the students observe a positive behavior, have them write it down on a note and place it in a box labeled *Caught You.* At the end of the week, read the notes aloud. The class will enjoy hearing positive comments from their peers.

## Setting Goals

Achieving goals is one way to boost one's self-esteem. Setting class goals brings the class together and makes the students recognize that they are members of a group. Discuss what a goal is, what you do to work towards a goal, and how you know when you have reached it. Have students brainstorm a list of goals that they think would be appropriate for the class. Identify the goals that seem to be common goals. Then let the students vote on two or three goals. Acknowledge any effort towards achievement of a goal. Reward the class as it completes a goal.

## Awards

Everyone loves to receive awards for accomplishments. Use the award certificate (page 93) any time you feel a student deserves one.

## Star of the Week

Help develop your students' confidence by making them feel special. Feature a student as Star of the Week. This week the featured student will receive a set of signed positive notes from the class. Have a box labeled *Star Notes* for the students to place their notes in. Post the instructions in a place where everyone can see them. Each student is responsible for participating in the program. Announce who the Star of the Week is and provide each student with a blank index card. You may want to read the notes before giving them to the class star to make sure there aren't any negative ones.

### *Instructions*

1. Write a validation sentence about the star of the week. Use these sentence starters.

   I respect you for . . .

   I admire you for . . .

   I am proud of you for . . .

   I am glad that you . . .

   I appreciate you for . . .

   I was pleased when you . . .

2. Sign your name at the bottom of the card, decorate it, and drop it in the star box.

# COOPERATIVE LEARNING

Cooperative learning strategies can be used to maximize your students' learning and to give them opportunities to learn to work together. Cooperative learning is more than just working in groups. It is the students working together to accomplish group goals while still being held individually accountable for learning. When

> Taking an interest in what students are thinking and doing is often a much more powerful form of encouragement than praise.
> —Robert Martin

students work in cooperative groups, they explore, experiment, and create while developing social, communication, and leadership skills. There are many benefits to cooperative learning. Students learn important social skills and responsibility. They learn leadership skills and they learn to evaluate their own work as well as the group's work. When assigning cooperative groups, include students of all ability levels in each group. Here are a few things to keep in mind.

## Planning

You'll want to find out if your class has worked in cooperative groups before or if this is their first cooperative learning experience. If they have no previous experience, it may be helpful to start off by working in pairs and gradually building up to 4–5 members. Here are some things you will need to decide before a lesson.

**Group Size**—Decide on what size group is best for the particular activity.

**Roles**—Decide if group members will have assigned roles and determine which roles will be needed.

**Materials**—Decide what materials are needed.

**Instructional Task**—Decide what concept or skill will be emphasized.

**Responsibility**—Decide what the group will be responsible for. Decide what each student will be responsible for.

**TIP!**

*Let your students know that you believe in them.*

**Social Skill Task**—Decide which social skills will be practiced.

**Evaluation**—Decide on a way to evaluate groups and individuals.

### Group Roles

Assigning roles to each student in a cooperative group helps keep everyone involved and responsible. Roles will differ with each activity. Here are some examples.

**Coach**—This person makes sure everyone in the group is participating. This person can represent the group if they need help from the teacher.

**Materials Manager**—This person is responsible for gathering any needed supplies.

**Reporter**—This person shares the group's work with the class.

**Recorder**—This person writes down the group's decisions when only one product is to be turned in by the group.

**Reader**—This person reads aloud to the group.

### Challenging Students

Students need to work cooperatively, so it is important to plan activities that challenge all students. Cooperative groups facilitate learning by providing students with opportunities to apply their particular intellectual and learning strengths to a variety of situations. Recognize that not all students learn the same way. Research Dr. Howard Gardner's multiple intelligence theory. Refer to *Multiple Intelligences Creative Teaching in the Fifth-Grade Classroom* (Frank Schaffer Publications, 1999) for assistance in applying these theories.

### Individual Responsibility

Build strategies into every cooperative group lesson to hold each student individually responsible for his or her learning. Try some of these ideas.

> **TIP!**
>
> *Fill the classroom with student-made displays and bulletin boards that express encouragement, recognition, and enthusiasm for learning.*

**Involve Everyone**—Keep everyone involved by randomly calling on group members to report progress or present projects.

**Self-evaluation**—Have students evaluate themselves and their groups after each cooperative group activity. Have them write responses to questions such as *How did I help my group? How can I be a better group member?*

**Follow-up**—Have each member do a similar assignment individually after a group has completed an assignment.

**Tests**—Individual tests and quizzes can have a place in a cooperative learning classroom. Every activity doesn't need to be followed by a test, but periodic examinations will remind students of their responsibilities to learn.

# MOTIVATING STUDENTS

Students who are motivated want to come to school, want to pay attention, and want to do their best. In order to be motivated, students must be in a classroom where they:

- Feel Safe—Students need to be free of worry about their physical or emotional well-being. Avoid any type of sarcasm which students may interpret as ridicule. Speak to students privately when they have grade concerns or they misbehave. Do not tolerate any student-to-student ridicule or threats.

- Feel Involved—Ask for student input when possible. Frequently ask them about their learning experiences.

- Feel Cared For—Students need to feel that they are cared for by both the teacher and other students. Learn their names as soon as possible. Greet each student every day. Listen sincerely when students express themselves.

- Feel Successful—Avoid giving meaningless praise. Give specific feedback instead. Let students know when you've noticed any specific improvements. Post their work in the classroom.

# TEACHER-TO-TEACHER-ADVICE

## When A Student Is Absent

When a student is absent, he or she can miss a lot of class work. Place a folder on his or her desk labeled "Work Done In Your Absence." Throughout the day, add papers and information to the folder. At the end of the day, slip the folder into a resealable plastic bag decorated to make it look inviting and leave it for the student. Add to it each day the student is absent.

You can foster more personal responsibility in the class if you assign a student or a team of two students to gather the materials an absent student will need to catch up. Call them the mentors. The mentors are also responsible for going through the package with the student who returns to explain any information that needs to be discussed.

## When You are Absent

Even if you have enjoyed perfect health before you started working as a teacher, you will get sick. You are exposed to lots of germs in a school. Usually by your third year of teaching your immunity is built enough so that you don't catch every cold or other virus that walks through your classroom door.

In addition, in-service educational experiences may be scheduled during the school day so that you must be away from your classroom.

Your school district may have a service that arranges for substitutes or you may have to find your own. At the beginning of the year, find what you need to do by asking another teacher or your school secretary.

Prepare a substitute kit and keep it in an easily accessible place. Make sure the students know where it is kept so they can assist the substitute. Include in the kit a copy of the form on page 94 to communicate with your "sub."

## Child Abuse

In many states, teachers are required by law to report any suspicion of child abuse. Proving abuse is not your responsibility, but reporting suspicions of abuse is. Some schools will follow up a teacher's suspicions, other schools require the teacher to act alone. Check with your school or district about your legal responsibilities.

## Personality—Let Yours Shine

Great teachers can also be artists, musicians, multiple-language speakers, writers, athletes, community activists, or any of a number of talented people outside of the classroom. We must remember to bring our talents to school. Remember to bring your personality into the classroom. Not only will you enjoy your job more, but your students will benefit as well.

## Attitude is Everything

Sometimes just getting through one day seems like a struggle. You get up late, the drive to school is treacherous, inclement weather causes the students to stay in all day, you forgot you had lunchroom duty, the principal is going to observe your teaching, and when you get to school you discover you put on different-colored socks. Days like these will happen. You have to know that things aren't always going to go the way you planned. This is okay. For this kind of day, it is good to prepare some fun and enjoyable activities that involve a lot of laughing. Incorporate them into your instructional day when you need to lighten the atmosphere. Whether you stay with your original daily plans or wing an activity, try to make the best of your choice. There are teachable moments in everything that you do.

> **Take rest, a field that has rested gives a bountiful crop.**
> **—Ovid**

**91**

### Take Care of Yourself

Teaching is a consuming job. It is easy to find yourself spending every waking minute thinking about your students, your classroom, and what you are going to do next, and every sleeping minute dreaming about school. There will be days when you are working ten or more hours just to keep up with your job responsibilities. This is a quick way to burn out. Pace yourself. Make yourself leave after you have worked eight hours. Exercise regularly and take some classes that are not related to the field of education. Keep your life in balance, and you will be the most effective teacher you can be.

**TIP!**

*Give yourself at least one weekend day for recreation—no school work!*

Every second we live is a new and unique moment of the universe, a moment that never was before and never will be again. And what do we teach our children in school? We teach them that 2 and 2 makes 4 and that Paris is the capital of France. When will we also teach them what they are? We should say to each of them: Do you know what you are? You are a marvel. You are unique. In all the world there is no other child exactly like you. In the millions of years that have passed there has never been a child like you. And look at your body what a wonder it is! Your legs, your arms, your cunning fingers, the way you move! You may become a Shakespeare, a Michelangelo, a Beethoven. You have the capacity for anything. Yes, you are a marvel. And when you grow up can you then harm another who is, like you, a marvel? You must cherish one another. You must work—we must all work—to make this world worthy of its children.

**—Pablo Casals**

**92**

# AWARD CERTIFICATE

IS A 5TH GRADE STAR

YOU HAVE EARNED SPECIAL RECOGNITION FOR

PRESENTED ON: _____

SIGNED _____

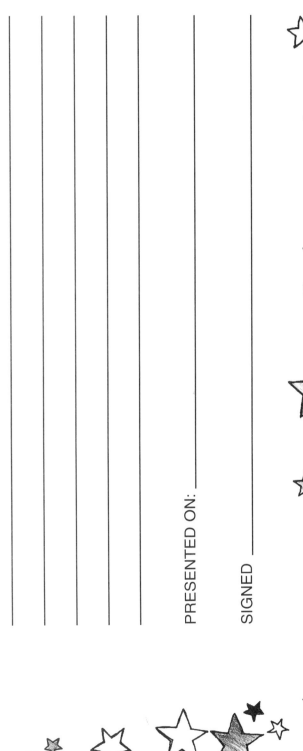

# SUBSTITUTE INFORMATION SHEET

Teacher _____     Room # _____

Location of Lesson Plan Books _____

## Daily Schedule

Time                    Subject/Activity

_____           _____

_____           _____

_____           _____

_____           _____

_____           _____

_____           _____

_____           _____

_____           _____


Lunchtime _____     Breaktime _____

Dependable Student Helpers

_____     _____     _____

Neighboring Teacher _____     Room Number _____

Emergency Drill Procedures

_____

_____

_____

Other Information

_____

_____

_____